VAN TIL

VAN TIL
Defender of
the Faith

An Authorized Biography

WILLIAM WHITE, JR.

THOMAS NELSON PUBLISHERS
Nashville   New York

Copyright 1979 by William White, Jr.

All rights reserved under International and Pan-American Conventions. Published in Nashville, Tennessee, by Thomas Nelson Inc., Publishers and simultaneously in Don Mills, Ontario, by Thomas Nelson & Sons (Canada) Limited. Manufactured in the United States of America.

Library of Congress Cataloging in Publication Data

White, William, 1934–
    Van Til, defender of the faith.

    1.   Van Til, Cornelius, 1895–   2.   Theologians—
United States—Biography.   I.   Title.
BX9225.V37W47   285'.731'0924   [B]   79-9732
ISBN 0-8407-5670-4

CONTENTS

ACKNOWLEDGMENTS

The author first became intrigued with the idea of writing a biography of Dr. Cornelius Van Til in 1957 when he began to study with the famed professor. Over the intervening twenty years, hundreds of interviews were held with members of the Van Til family and many of Van Til's colleagues in the Netherlands, Canada, and the United States, as well as with former students and readers of his writings dispersed as far as South Africa and Japan. In addition, thousands of pages were read which had been written by, about, or against him. Finally, many hours of tape recordings were made of discussions with Dr. and Mrs. Van Til in their stone house in the rolling hills of suburban Philadelphia.

The publisher and author wish to thank Earl and Thelma Van Til, Sam Van Til, and many other members of the Van Til family; Rev. Paul Woolley; Mrs. Margaret Stonehouse; Rev. Roy Oliver; and Dr. Robert Knudsen. Special thanks goes to Robert T. Tuten and Harry Schat with whom the author discussed details of this project for over a decade; most special thanks goes to Rev. Henry Coray who acted as editor and who made more corrections and valuable suggestions than can be listed.

VAN TIL

PREFACE

In his profile of Albert Einstein, C. P. Snow says the great scientist used the word *God* so often that people were deceived. "When he spoke of God, he did not mean what a religious believer means. He believed in Spinoza's God 'who reveals himself in the harmony of all being, not in a God who concerns himself with the fate and actions of men.' "

According to Snow, Einstein spent forty years in a quest for what he himself called a "unified field theory." That is, his brilliant mind explored the universe trying to find out if there was a key to the puzzle of the existence of matter and of life. He longed to catch a glimpse into "the eternal secrets of nature." He failed signally. Why? The answer to the question is significant. Professor Snow tells you "He believed each single decision that he took in life *came from within himself*" (italics ours).

There you have it. Dr. Einstein, like multitudes of pundits, including scientists, philosophers and theologians, believed in the autonomy of the human intellect. He was persuaded that his brain had sufficient power to figure out the riddle of the universe, the unifying principle of spirit and matter.

But instead of starting his investigation with
the living and true God, he relied on himself. Result: His search ended in a cul-de-sac, leaving him
frustrated, disappointed, pathetic.

This philosophy is concretely expressed in a recent issue of *Time:* "In a sense God, the personal,
omnipotent deity of Christianity, has been dying
for centuries. . . . It is the twentieth century, the
age of technological miracles, that has seen the
triumph of Enlightenment, and the apparent
banishment of God from the universe, even, thanks
to Freud, from the human soul."

Now the scene changes but the scenario remains
the same. Proud Goliath, protected from head to toe
with heavy armor and comfortably deployed behind a shield-bearer, comes forth from bivouac to
defy the army of the God of Israel. An unknown
shepherd youth advances to intercept him. The
giant greets him with loud jibes and sneers.

Where is David's armor? He has experimented
with King Saul's helmet and coat of mail, and has
rejected both. "I cannot go with them, for I have not
tried them." You see, he refused to fight the Lord's
battle in Saul's armor.

A young theologian originally out of Holland
stands before the junior class in apologetics at
Princeton Theological Seminary. It is to be his first
lecture. The year is 1928. He is about to begin a new
tack in the field of American apologetics. (The word
apologetics derives from 1 Peter 3:15: ". . . be ready
always to give an answer [an *apologia,* an intelli-
gent, verbal defense] to every man that asketh you a
reason of the hope that is in you. . . .") He has

carefully analyzed the conventional approach used by the majority of American Christian apologists, weighed it in the balance of Scripture, and found it wanting. Good men and true, the average apologists may be, but, unfortunately, they are fighting the Lord's battle in Saul's armor.

Generally, their argument, following Butler in his *Analogy*, runs like this: One is able to prove the existence of God on rational grounds. The very presence of a creation presupposes a Creator. There is a design in this universe, therefore there must be a Designer. Obviously, there is a plan behind living matter, so it follows there has got to be a Planner. The argument sounds plausible, does it not?

Cornelius Van Til's difficulty with this line of reasoning is that he sees it as a syllogism built on a false premise, the law of probability.

A man buttons his shirt. In all probability every button is in its proper place. Alas, a second look shows him he has made a bad mistake. He began by placing the first button in the second buttonhole. The whole effort therefore calls for undoing and realignment.

Van Til reasons that in apologetics to employ the launching pad of the naked intellect instead of the launching pad of Scripture is to give away too much to the unregenerate. With Moses, he is convinced that all thinking must begin where the Bible does: "In the beginning God. . . .", otherwise all is chaos. Like David, he believes that "With thee [God] is the fountain of life: in thy light shall we see light" (Ps. 36:9); otherwise all is darkness. Like Amos, he has accepted the proposition that God

"declareth unto man what is his [man's] thought"
(Amos 4:13); otherwise the human mind is operating in a vacuum. Following Paul, he concludes that
we are not "sufficient of ourselves to think any
thing as of ourselves; but our sufficiency is of God"
(2 Cor. 3:5); if not, then we are on an intellectual
treadmill. To concede that the mind of the thinker
can by searching find out about God, or discover
truth, be it Plato's or Spinoza's or Einstein's, is in
effect to fight the Lord's battle in Saul's armor.

   This, in abridged form, is Dr. Van Til's position.
Curiously, it has made him a storm center of controversy. He has been praised, condemned,
quoted, misquoted, represented, misrepresented,
understood, misunderstood, loved, hated, explored, ignored. Above the lightning, thunder,
wind, and hail he has stood his ground coolly and
calmly; inflexible in his stance, he is the most flexi-
ble of humans in his willingness to listen to criticism. He, like Luther, is "bold before men, humble
before God."

   This is the story of Cornelius Van Til.

CHAPTER 1

"Kees"

The springtime sun rose brightly and shone on the flowers and the tender shoots in the fields and gardens. Only a few steely-gray clouds, so characteristic of the Dutch sky, promised the coming of the rain. It was a lovely Friday, the third of May. Children looked forward to going home from school, workmen from their jobs, and farmers from their fields. Farm women busily prepared for the hustle and bustle of the coming market day, when the jostling crowds, the open stalls, and the sounds of church bells and street organs would all come together in the villages and towns spread across the dark polder land from the North Sea to the German border.

Nothing spectacular or noteworthy in the annals of history happened in the Low Countries on that lovely spring day in 1895. However, in the solid old farmhouse of Ite Van Til, with its attached barn and red tile roof, Ite's good wife, Klazina, gave birth to their sixth child, Kornelis. True, the chroniclers of men and nations may never note the birth of the little Dutch boy nor his later career, but hundreds of thousands of God's people around the world have read his writings and, through his pronouncement of the gospel and defense of the faith, have taken heart to follow the Lord Jesus Christ in the turmoil and unbelief of the present century.

To most Americans, the Netherlands, "where the broad ocean leans against the land," is identified with names such as Erasmus, Rembrandt, Van Gogh, Vermeer, Stevin, Huygens, and Anne Frank; with endless canals and waterways; with *Hans Brinker and the Silver Skates;* with the Puritans who left in order to settle in the new world across the Atlantic; and with the small boy who when there was a leak in the dike held back the sea water with his hand (a myth that always causes a hearty laugh from the sons and daughters of Holland).

This tiny, densely populated nation has contributed more to the difficult fields of philosophy and theology than most people are aware of. "Holland is one of the traditional lands of freedom," wrote Havelock Ellis. "It is the home of independent intellect; of free religion when every other country in Europe was closed to these manifestations of the spirit." It may not be an overstatement to assert that what ancient Greece donated to philosophy and ancient Rome to jurisprudence, the Netherlands has given to theology.

From the early spring of the Reformation, the Dutch love of metaphysics, the branch of philosophy that probes the nature of first principles and problems of ultimate reality—Einstein's "unified field theory"—found expression in the rise of innovative religious groups. Those who participated were known as Brethren of the Common Life. They conducted their services in the *Null*, or "low" form of speech. From the womb of this movement two famous personalities came forth: Erasmus, the first scholar to edit a Greek Version of the New Testament, and a simple monk, Thomas à Kempis, whose *Imitation of Christ*, George Eliot states, "is the chronicle of a solitary, hidden anguish, struggle, trust, and triumph. It remains at all times a lasting record of human needs and consolations."

Both Catholics and Protestants owe a lasting debt to Dutch thinkers. Prior to the Council of Trent (1545–1563), the Roman Church had no common system of doctrine. And the cold, wet, harsh environment of the lowlands, together with its fierce struggle against the sea and the elements, provided just the right soil for the seeds of a robust Calvinism passed down from Geneva. Reformed churches sprang up, Christian schools were founded, a Protestant newspaper was widely circulated, a Protestant political party began to exert a vital influence on the eleven provinces. The leavening power of the Reformed faith injected iron and steel into the character of Dutch citizens, stimulating personal and social responsibility and a love for democracy. Wherever Reformed theology took root downward, it bore fruit upward.

In the post-Reformation period, when population upheavals and political pressures forced not a few natives of the Netherlands to emigrate to other shores, they carried with them a passionate dedication to the principles of a free society. This spirit has had a salutary impact on life in Canada and in the United States, an influence that has proven far out of proportion to the number of emigrants.

One prominent feature of Dutch life in the past was the strict ordering of one's personal affairs in all areas of life, called in Dutch, *verzuiling*, which means something like "columnization." In actual practice it traditionally meant that a Dutch Protestant went to a Protestant church, sent his children to a Protestant school, made sure his taxes went to support Protestant institutions, read a Protestant newspaper, joined a Protestant club, and voted for a Protestant political party. A Roman Catholic or a nonreligious person followed a similar pattern. Thus, the Netherlands had possibly the most ideologically consistent social system in the western world. Perhaps the negative side of the tradition was that three families, a Protestant, a Catholic, and a nonreligious, could all live on the same block of the same narrow street for a decade and not even know each other.

On the positive side, the practice engendered a far higher knowledge about the Bible and the outreach of Christianity than could be found in an equivalent population in England or the United States. Out of this strangely columnar society have come some of the world's best trained and most dedicated Christian thinkers.

In the northernmost section of Holland lies the province of Groningen. Here lives a race of Germanic-speaking people known as the Fries (pronounced Frees). They are a strong, proud, independent-minded folk, distinct from other Hollanders but tightly bound to them in interests and destiny. Early in the Christian era, the Fries were subjugated by the Romans and later by the Germans and Franks successively. In 1523, under William of Orange, they regained their liberty. In World War II, they, as well as the other inhabitants of the lowlands, stood out as one of the most stubborn pockets of resistance in all of Europe against the Nazi invaders.

On May 3, 1895, Cornelius Van Til entered the world in the village of Grootegast. A strain of Fries blood ran in the Van Til stock. The grandfather, Reinder, was a man of varied talents: He made his living as the owner and manager of a tavern, he thought as a Christian philosopher, and he taught his family and friends as a theologian.

In his day the Reformed Church of the Netherlands split over the issue of baptismal regeneration. The majority of the leaders and members believed that children of the covenant were regenerated, presumably, by virtue of natural birth in a pious home. Thus, infant baptism became confirmation of the child's salvation. The minority, on the other hand, reasoned that although covenant children ought to be baptized, nurtured in the bosom of the church, and given its privileges, they must, by sovereign mercy exercise true repentance and make personal appropriation of the Savior and His redemption. The innkeeper identified himself with the latter party, the *Afscheiding*. The *Afscheiding* were cruelly barred from worshiping in formal church buildings. In consequence, they had to hold their services in barns or public buildings. This they did resolutely and cheerfully until they were able to put up their own churches.

Reinder's son, Ite, a towering mound of muscles, wore a snowy, flowing beard and bore the image of an Old Testament patriarch. Like most residents of Groningen he was a dairyman, breeding and trading cattle. Also, his forty-acre farm produced garden vegetables, hay, and flax.

The nineteenth-century Dutch believed in large families. Ite and Klazina Van Til contributed eight children to the world, seven boys and a daughter. Tragically, a childhood accident took the life of the girl while she was still very young.

Cornelius was the sixth son. His mother, he will tell you, remembers him as a fussy baby. In his early childhood his chief delights were to play in a sandbox under a spreading willow tree and to pass the nights with a hired hand sleeping high in a hayloft in his father's barn. He acquired the nickname Kees (pronounced Case), a designation still used by his close friends.

Like any child in all good Reformed families, Kees was sent to a Christian school. Accompanied by his brother, Jacob, he trudged two miles to the school house. En route they frequently stopped to pole vault various and sundry obstacles and the smaller canals.

It was the custom for Dutch children to wear pointed wooden shoes, or *klompa*. During school hours students were forbidden to remove these shoes. There was method in the mandate. The authorities knew about a certain practice carried on by hotheaded youth. It seems that sometimes when altercations took place tempers would flare, fists would fly, and the combatants would remove their *klompa* and whack each other over the head. Such action was definitely out-of-bounds.

Both in the Van Til home and in the Christian school, the Bible occupied a central place. Family worship, including catechetical instruction, was an important factor in the spiritual development of the children. Cornelius still recalls and recites with feeling the answer to the first question in the Heidelberg Catechism, which is: "What is your only comfort in life and death?"

That I with body and soul, both in life and death, am not my own, but belong to my faithful Savior Jesus Christ, who with His precious blood has fully satisfied for all my sins, and redeemed me from all the power of the devil, and so preserved me, that without the will of my Father in heaven not a hair can fall from my head; indeed, that all things must work together for my salvation. Wherefore, by His Holy Spirit, He also assures me of eternal life, and makes me heartily willing and ready to live unto Him.

One can visualize the Van Til family on the Lord's Day walking solemnly to the house of prayer with the children wearing black, wooden *klompa*. Mr. Van Til would tolerate no lightness or foolishness on the way or during the service. He and his loved ones gathered with others of like precious faith to worship the great King in the beauty of

holiness. Nothing was to detract from the reverence
due the Lord of glory.

If on the way home it happened to be raining,
tiny snails would work their way out of the
ground—to the delight of the children. Then Father
would relax and smile as the boys would repeat an
ancient Dutch proverb, "You can't drop salt on
every snail." Moral: "Don't spread yourself too
thin: life is too short."

There you have the ingredients that combined to
shape godly lives in the home of Ite and Klazina
Van Til. To their offspring they bequeathed a love
valued far above rubies, a pattern of strict but im-
partial discipline, exposure to a rich heritage of
Calvinistic theology, a God-centered life and world
view, and minds filled with fragrant recollections
of a happy home.

One may readily understand the nostalgic mood
of Cornelius Van Til if, now in the sunset of his life,
he often reaches back and lives over again those
golden years in Groningen, and repeats the wistful
words of the poet:

Ah, fields beloved in vain,
Where once my careless childhood stray'd,
A stranger yet to pain:
I feel the gates that from ye blow
A momentary bliss bestow.

CHAPTER 2

The Immigrants

Soon after Kees had begun his schooling, the Van Til family moved to the village of De Leek, located on the border of the provinces of Groningen and Friesland. There on the twenty-acre farm, Ite was able to improve his lot by raising in great abundance carrots, cabbages, potatoes, and cauliflower. The damp rich soil also yielded peat, or *baggel*, which the family wrested from the ground and sold at a handsome price. *Baggel* is a mossy substance, usually cut into blocks eight inches square, three or four inches in thickness, and used for both fuel and fertilizer.

One of the supreme joys of the children was the anticipation of spring; it meant the gathering of large, sweet, succulent strawberries. These they ate with zest, sometimes as they came fresh from the earth, sometimes converted by Klazina into delectable pies or luscious tarts.

The Van Tils had not lived long in De Leek when Ite made a momentous decision. One of the older boys, Hendrik, was drafted into the Dutch army and stationed at Assen in the province of Drenta. The specter of long military service for Hendrik and the other sons cast a shadow over the home. Mr. and Mrs. Van Til realized the prospect of watching the lads leave home, one by one, to take up soldiering. Who then would do the farming?

With his father's consent, Reinder, eleven years older than Kees, married and with his bride left Holland for America. They settled on a farm near Highland, Indiana, ten miles south of Hammond. Reinder rented forty acres at five dollars an acre, bought two mules, and was in business. He wrote his parents urging them to follow him to the land of opportunity.

In the spring of 1905, with conflicting emotions, the Van Til family, minus Hendrik, prepared to leave their fatherland. Their roots were deep in the soil there. The move meant parting with relatives, friends, acquaintances, and giving up church ties as well as cultural patterns and traditions of long standing. But in the mind of Ite the reported advantages of life in the new world, set against the uncertainties of continuing life in Holland, tipped the scales in favor of the change. Having put his hand on the plough, there was no turning back.

They went to Rotterdam by train, boarded a Holland-American Line steamer and sailed for New York. Their ship arrived on May 19, 1905, thirteen days after Kees's tenth birthday. Mrs. Van Til, who was thought to have had a touch of tuberculosis, experienced such an improvement in condition while on board that she appeared to be in perfect health by the time the vessel docked. Incidentally, she lived to the age of seventy-three.

In New York City the family took passage on an Erie Railroad train that would take them to Hammond. It proved to be a gruelling, tortuous journey. (The old Erie Railroad trains were never noted for their speed. It was rumored that once a certain man, discouraged with his lot, decided to take his life; he lay down on the Erie tracks and died of starvation!) The twenty-six-hour trip was especially hard on little Siepko (later Sydney), at the time a babe in arms.

They reached Hammond at last. Reinder met them at the station. Great was the rejoicing at the reunion. Reinder put the weary travelers and their effects in a huge horse-drawn wagon. They were jolted over ten miles of unpaved highways to Highland. The boys were full of wonder and excitement at the sights and sounds of American rural life: the lowing cattle, the sleek-looking horses, the immense barns and silos, the neat farm houses, the flat, wooded country.

Highland in those days was not exactly a metropolis. Six landmarks graced the community landscape: a post office, a Christian Reformed church, a school house, a blacksmith shop, a railroad roundhouse, and a saloon.

Reinder had arranged for the family to move into a rented house. So began the period of adjustment to a new environment, a new culture, and a strange language.

The Van Tils wasted no time joining the church. Its minister, a Pastor Sherda—often referred to as "the domine" (master)—they found to be a godly and compassionate man. He took special interest in the Van Til boys and was of inestimable aid counseling Kees about his future plans.

The brothers attended a two-room school house. They picked up the English language rapidly. Kees, who was placed back in first grade, mastered the language so well that within the year he moved up to the fifth grade. The teacher nicknamed Kees *Big Klompa* and Jacob *Little Klompa*. Later, when one of their older brothers, Klaas, enrolled, the teacher called him, *Brother of the two Klompas*. The other two brothers did not attend school but instead helped their father with the farming.

At first Ite tried to grow onions. The experiment failed. The onions bolted to seed, became "stiff-necked," and were unusable.

He enjoyed better success raising small cucumbers. These he sold to Libby and McNeil for fifty cents a bushel. This transaction still generates a rise of anger in Cornelius. "I shudder," he says, "when I think of the back-breaking labor that went into every bushel for that miserable price."

On the whole, however, conditions were an improvement over those in the Netherlands. Ite was able to cultivate various kinds of vegetables and to make wine from the wild grapes on the land.

Kees' love of the soil did not diminish one iota in his new Indiana home. He was never happier than when breaking ground with a hoe, weeding, harrowing, and harvesting. Regularly, he and his father would take the fruit of their toil and personally market it, moving from house to house in neighboring towns. One of the very responsive communities turned out to be Whiting, a city ten miles to the north of Highland. Whiting was a pioneer in the oil-producing industry and quickly gained the reputation of being a boom town. Van Til loved the trips into Whiting, the selling door to door, and the big beef sandwiches and icy cold drinks at day's end.

Ite secured farm supplies from Sears and Roebuck. Because Kees had advanced so nicely in his grasp of the difficult new language, his father put him in charge of communicating with the company in matters of buying, selling, and clearing up inevitable misunderstandings. On one occasion he was instrumental in returning to the store part of an over-supply of dynamite.

Kees was as fond of animals as he was of the soil. He enjoyed leading his favorite horse, Nellie, to the village blacksmith to have her shod. "It always fascinated me to watch the blacksmith in action, to listen to the hissing sounds as he'd plunge a hot iron into a pail of water, and to watch the sparks fly from the anvil when he'd hammer a horseshoe into shape."

So the adjustment to American ways, mores, and the general tempo of life was effected, gradually by the parents, swiftly by their sons.

After ten years of residence in Highland, Ite thought it wise to move the family to Munster, Indiana.

Two events unfolded that profoundly affected the future of Kees. He met the daughter of a nearby neighbor, Rena Klooster, an exceptionally attractive girl with lovely manners and a sunny disposi-

tion; and so began a courtship that eventually was
to culminate in a wedding and stretch out over fifty
beautiful years.

The second development altered the course of his
life and the lives of thousands of others, as well as
the cause of Christ's universal kingdom, though
Cornelius knew it not at the time. He was called to
the Christian ministry.

CHAPTER 3
The Divine Call Tested

To Kees Van Til the summons to proclaim the gospel came not in a momentary, dramatic flash—like a chain of lightning streaking across the sky. Rather, the experience could be defined as a compulsion, a steady pull, a developing persuasion. In the secular world lived a society of men, women, and youth standing in desperate need of the good tidings of great joy. The desire to reach the weary and heavy laden with the liberating Word and to build up the Lord's covenant people took strong hold on Kees, creating a restlessness of soul. Eventually, he arrived at the conviction that he could say, with Paul, ". . . woe is unto me, if I preach not the gospel!" (1 Cor. 9:16).

Charles Haddon Spurgeon used to give this advice to the students in his college: "Young men, if you can possibly stay out of the ministry, do so." What he meant of course was, "Unless the prophetic urge grips you, do something else with your life."

The decision to forsake farming and take steps to prepare for the holy ministry was by no means easy for the nineteen-year-old Van Til. But he would be the last person on earth to plead, "Lord, here am I, send somebody else." The haunting words of Isaiah, "Lord, here am I, send me," (6:8) were engraved on his heart. He set his face like flint to carry out what he believed to be the will of God.

For years, Grand Rapids, Michigan, had functioned as the Jerusalem, the nerve center, of the Christian Reformed movement. In that bustling Dutch community, Calvin Preparatory School and College and Calvin Seminary had been founded to train young men and young women for their life's work.

Kees left Munster and entered the Preparatory School in the autumn of 1914, the year Europe was plunged into World War I.

The first months in Grand Rapids left the student from the Hoosier state discouraged and despondent in spite of his love of learning. A bad case of homesickness afflicted him. His thoughts constantly strayed back to the close-knit Van Til family. He missed the company of sweet Rena much more than he had anticipated. He yearned to return to Munster and the good earth, the horses and cattle, the kiss of the turf, the joy of watching God at work in the fields and gardens. At a particularly low point in his morale, his faith wavered and the certainty of his calling lost ground. He considered seriously giving up his studies and going back home.

Cornelius Van Til will tell you candidly he was wrong to think of quitting school. In his mellow years he has become somewhat of a cracker barrel philosopher as well as a metaphysician of note.

"Never make an important decision when you're tired or discouraged," he will say with a twinkle in his brown eyes. "I almost did once, and but for the grace of God I'd have gotten into hot water."

Three factors kept him on an even keel. From Rena's letters he received considerable comfort and encouragement. Again, he was the first of his family to strive for a formal education. His parents and brothers were proud to know that *Big Klompa* was getting ready to be ordained. How could he hold his head up if in a moment of weakness he threw in the proverbial towel? Finally, a second cousin, Herman Moes, "a brother born for adversity," befriended him at that critical stage, talked with him at length, and was instrumental in getting him out of the Slough of Despond. By the time the Christmas season rolled around, Van Til had canceled all ideas of interrupting his preseminary education.

Enormous relief followed in the wake of that decision.

Still, his preparatory and college years proved to be periods of testing in the crucible, mentally and physically. Because of the financial pinch, he was obliged to find part-time work. Room and board cost him four dollars a week. To supplement the limited amount of scholarship aid supplied by the Christian Reformed Church Student Fund, he secured an assignment doing janitorial service in the dormitories.

While many other students spent their leisure hours enjoying sports, courtship, and the social whirl, Kees, with no little pleasure and excitement, was delving into the labyrinthine treatises of Soc-

rates, Plato, Aristotle, Kant, Hegel, and Schopenhauer.

Philosophy is a branch of learning that deals with
the abstract. It is a source of puzzlement to thinkers
and writers who, like John Bunyan, work with the
idiom of the concrete. To Cornelius Van Til, however, it holds a strange and wonderful fascination.
Possibly this interest was because of the influence
of some of the scholars connected with the *Afscherd-
ing,* or because of the things he picked up from his
grandfather, a clear thinker in his own right. At any
rate, the presuppositions, syllogisms, and a
hundred other details that leave many, like
Mohammed's coffin, suspended between heaven
and earth, early became Kees Van Til's nectar and
ambrosia. Perhaps, even then, his analytical mind
was putting together bits and pieces for the structure of a Christian philosophy that would one day
challenge the presuppositions of non-Christian
scholars.

CHAPTER 4
The Farmer Scholar

During Cornelius Van Til's years of preseminary training, the quality of the teaching at the Grand Rapids preparatory school ranked high. Some of the seminary professors doubled on the faculty. So-called "practical courses" had not yet come into vogue. The founders of the institution had drawn from the pattern of the curriculum taught in Holland. There was little margin for individual diversion. There were no electives.

Two of *Big Klompa's* favorite teachers were Professor Klaas Scholland, under whom he studied classical Greek for four years, and Professor Van Andel, an instructor in Dutch history and literature. The latter, the students used to say, was "a real character." He would make an effort, whenever possible, to avoid the drudgery of Dutch declensions and conjugations by surveying in quick, enthusiastic bursts distinctive features of Flemish art and history. Musically gifted, he derived unalloyed pleasure from playing the organ and leading his classes in the singing of folk songs. One day somebody took him to task for his lack of mastery of the Dutch grammar. Screwing his face into a frown he responded acidly, "What? I gave them all A's, didn't I?"

Today, Dr. Van Til tells how Van Andel fired the imagination of his pupils and helped increase their appreciation for the greatness of the country of their forebears. He would recount the story of the Dutch armed forces in their life-and-death struggle to overcome Spanish rule. At the climax of the Eighty Years War between the two nations, Holland's chances for liberation appeared bleak indeed. Skeptics said of the cause of the Netherlands: *"radeloos, radaloss, en radalel,"* "without possibility, senseless and hopeless." But under the gallant leadership of William the Silent of the House of Orange, the Dutch overpowered Spain's proud armada, the Silver Fleet, knocked out a smashing victory, and freed the oppressed people from their hated foe.

It was while he was a student at the Grand Rapids school that Kees began to read extensively the writings of the great Abraham Kuyper.

Dr. Kuyper (1837-1920) performed the work of ten average men. He was educated at the University of Leiden and the Leiden Divinity School at a time when German destructive biblical criticism was infiltrating the Dutch institutions. The movement was known as the *Aufklarung,* the Enlightenment. Young Kuyper fell victim to its appeal to the intellect. He went into the ministry a dedicated liberal preaching an emasculated gospel. Through a saintly woman in his congregation and the reading of a Christian novel, *The Heir of Redcliffe,* his eyes were opened to see the error of his doctrines against the beauty of the true Christ. He was converted, transformed within from center to circumference. From that point on, his rapier-like mind championed the cause of historic, supernatural Christianity.

The record of his achievements reads like a one man's *Who's Who*. He edited two newspapers, was elected to Parliament, founded the Free Reformed University of Amsterdam, helped organize the Christian Conservative Ministry, served with distinction as Prime Minister of the Netherlands from 1901 to 1905, taught classes and lectured at the university, and preached regularly. In addition, he managed in his leisure hours to write two hundred titled books, including three monumental volumes on *Gemene Gratia*, (common grace); an exposition of the Heidelberg Catechism; a *Theological Encyclopedia; Around the Ancient World,* the account of an extended tour of the Middle East; *Pro Rege, For Christ the King; To be Near unto God,* a marvelously rich and penetrating series of devotional messages now, unfortunately, out of print.

His principal thesis was that the Christianity set forth in the Bible is the one God-revealed religion, and that Calvinism is the clearest and most consistent expression of that religion—both in content and in its life-and-world presentation.

Cornelius Van Til freely admits that when it comes to the background for some of his formulations he stands on the shoulders of Abraham Kuyper. "Wanting to follow the Reformers, it was natural that I read and appreciated the works of those who before me likewise attempted to do so,"

he says. "I first used the works of Kuyper and
Bavinck. How basic and broad was their view! The
idea of Scripture, they said, must never be separated from its *message*."

It is true, Dr. Van Til takes guarded issue with
Abraham Kuyper on certain important points. As
Richard Gaffin, Jr., has indicated in *Jerusalem and
Athens*, Van Til, following Geerhardus Vos, chal-
lenges Kuyper's "leveling treatment of the biblical
authors," his "rejection of biblical theology not
only in name but in concept," and his "discon-
tinuity between biblical writers and the theological
activity of subsequent Christian generations." The
differences, however, in no way diminish his admiration, respect, and affection for Holland's most
illustrious statesman-theologian. The practical influence of that giant of a man may be seen not only
in Van Til's life of faith, but also in the slightly
old-fashioned, somewhat florid touches one may
discover in his sermons and the classical nuances in
some of his writings.

In his student days, Kees always looked forward
to the summer months on the farm with an elation
that bordered on euphoria. The days represented
reunion with his beloved family, resumption of
rugged but happy toil in the fields under a blazing
Indiana sun, and a chance to replenish his dwin-
dling financial resources. But above all this, they
meant blissful hours with Rena, in an outdoor
swing or ensconced in a shiny little surrey with the
fringe on top meandering along leafy country lanes
absolutely oblivious to the passing of time or the
tentative threat of an electric storm. The retired

professor of apologetics will heartily agree that "there's nothing half so sweet in life as love's young dream."

In 1921, Van Til enrolled at Calvin Theological Seminary. He hoped eventually to pastor a rural church, at least for a season.

Already he had acquainted himself not only with the Dutch and English languages but with Latin, Greek, and Hebrew as well. In intellectual stature and outlook, he had probably advanced beyond most of his classmates.

Here was a youth who in his early years in the Netherlands had been exposed to a "columnized" culture; that is, as a Dutch covenant child he had attended a strictly Protestant school, a Protestant church, read a Protestant newspaper, formed friendships with other Protestant children—in short, breathed Protestant air.

Nevertheless, the advantages had been in many ways wholesome. Products of this kind of environment know what they believe and why. They entertain a deep respect for authority. They realize from experience what discipline is. They are taught to try to view all phases and spheres of life through the eyes of God. They are aware that they are not swinging blindly through space without direction or goal.

After coming to America, Van Til's horizons had broadened. He was grateful for his years in the Netherlands, but now he knew he was to be involved with people existing in a complex, pluralistic society. All around him, acquaintances thought, felt, talked, vibrated on different wavelengths.

America had not yet recovered from the shattering explosion of World War I. Multitudes wandered in the valley of indecision—bewildered, confused, frustrated. He reflected, "How can I, Cornelius Van Til, a transplanted farmer, serve as a physician of value in a sick world? God help me to know."

In the Grand Rapids "school of the prophets," exceptionally able theologians held forth. Cornelius felt himself fortunate to be taking instruction from scholars like Louis Berkhof, Samuel Volbeda, William Heyns, Professor Ten Hor, and the outstanding Fries immigrant, W. H. Jellema, who himself had sat as a student at the feet of the renowned scholar, Josiah Royce.

In evangelical theological seminaries in America, there is a required course in homiletics, the art of preaching. The seminarian is called on to deliver an original sermon before a professor and the homiletics class. It is always somewhat of an ordeal, since the embryonic preacher must address a captive, critical congregation: his fellow classmates.

The hour arrived when it was Van Til's turn to preach, he chose for his text Revelation 3:20: "Behold, I stand at the door, and knock: if any man hear my voice, and open the door, I will come in to him, and will sup with him, and he with me."

If Coleridge's maxim, "In today, already walks tomorrow," is accurate, then it is possible that Cornelius Van Til's listeners may have seen in silhouette form the image of one whom God was to gift with a mind destined to operate like a Roman candle, and a heart burdened with great heaviness and continued sorrow for the lost.

CHAPTER 5
The Move to Princeton

In his well-known poem, "The Road not Taken," Robert Frost writes of the moment he came to a place in the forest where there was a parting of the ways. One road led through a yellow wood and was lost in the underbrush. The other had the better claim because it was grassy and wanted wear. He decided to follow the second trail. He concludes the poem with the lines:

> I shall be telling this with a sigh
> Somewhere ages and ages hence:
> Two roads diverged in a wood, and I—
> I took the one less traveled by,
> And that has made all the difference.[1]

His first, or junior year, at Calvin Seminary completed, Kees Van Til, like Frost, found himself standing at a crossroads. He could remain at Calvin, wind up his theological education there, and probably become a minister in a country church. Or he could apply for acceptance at Princeton Theolog-

---

[1] "The Road Not Taken," *New Republic*, vol. 34 (March 7, 1923).

ical Seminary in New Jersey and go on from there—to where? He was not at all sure. The desire to proclaim the gospel was still vibrant in him. As far as he could tell, either path would lead to the pulpit.

He weighed the problem prayerfully. Sentimentally, the case for staying on in Grand Rapids had a powerful appeal. He would be nearer his family and his sweetheart. He appreciated the excellent teaching of the Calvin scholars. He was perfectly at home rubbing shoulders with the Dutch population surrounding the seminary campus. In all probability he would feel more relaxed in the climate of the Midwest.

On the other hand, two factors joined to form a solid argument for making the move to the East. The first was the simple fact that students in Princeton Theological Seminary could also be admitted to Princeton University. At the time Princeton was rated as one of the foremost higher educational institutions in the States and boasted famous professors in the department of philosophy, men who had trained in Continental schools of thought.

The second argument loomed with equal force. On the faculty at Princeton Seminary were theologians mighty in the Scriptures: Geerhardus Vos, Casper Wister Hodge, William Park Armstrong, Robert Dick Wilson, Oswald T. Allis, and J. Gresham Machen. What could have more appeal than the chance to hone one's mind on the whetstone of scholarship that Princeton offered?

Van Til opted for Princeton.

Those who have ever studied in that quiet university town will swear there is no atmosphere on earth more conducive to meditation and concentration. Its broad streets, lined with stately elms and maples, its noble history stretching back to the Revolutionary War days, its lovely campuses so full of haunting lore, melt the strands of the community into one mystic think tank.

In the 1920s, the decade following the First World War, the universities in Germany were smouldering in the ashes of a broken intellectualism. The Ivy League schools of America, by contrast, stood out in bold relief as bastions of lively liberalism. Intellectually hungry young men from all over the world flocked to their halls to drink from the fountains of worldly wisdom. Harvard, Yale, and Princeton were magic words. People mentioned them almost in awe.

If the contrast between the German universities and the Ivy League schools was stark, the differences between Princeton University and Princeton Theological Seminary were just as pronounced. The university stood for relativism, the seminary for absolutism. The university acknowledged no ultimate authority; the seminary recognized the Scriptures of the Old and New Testaments as its final authority. The university held a mechanical, evolutionary view of the universe; the seminary believed this gigantic bubble to be the work of God's craftmanship. The university advocated an open-ended view of all learning; the seminary was convinced that Jesus Christ, God's mediatorial

King, was the touchstone of all truth and that in the Savior were laid up all the treasures of wisdom and knowledge.

The seminary administration approved Van Til's transfer from Calvin and enrolled him as a middler, or second year, classman. There was no problem, for students of Dutch extraction were generally rated a cut above others because of their intense Calvinistic training.

Kees was also permitted to register for courses in philosophy at the university. The head of the department, A. A. Bowman, was a committed personalist. Personalism is the theory of subjective idealism, which regards personality as the key to the interpretation of reality. Although Bowman and Van Til differed widely in their respective views, they nevertheless maintained a warm personal relationship.

During the twenties, a tidal wave of anti-intellectualism had engulfed the Christian community. Out of this trend grew an impatience with attempts to understand non-Christian thought. "Why not," it was argued, "present the simple gospel to the world and let it go at that?"

J. Gresham Machen was quick to analyze this line of reasoning and warn against it. He reminded Christian people that when Paul was presenting the gospel to the Stoic and Epicurean philosophers on the Aeropagus in Athens he showed his acquaintance with their own writers, quoting from Aratus and Cerinthus. Matthew Henry corroborates the point: "It appears that Paul was himself a scholar, but that human learning is both ornamental and serviceable to a gospel minister, especially for the convincing of those that are without; for it enables him to beat them at their own weapons, and to cut off Goliath's head with his own sword."

The two-edged sword that Van Til would one day wield was in point of fact forged not only in the reverent climate of Princeton Seminary but also in the rationalistic environment of Princeton University.

And so into this antithetical maelstrom of thought the youthful Hoosier plunged. It represented phase three of the preparation for life process: First, there had been the columnized cultural step in the Netherlands; second, the robust Calvinism of Grand Rapids; now the highly stylized strains of liberalism and conservatism coming together at Princeton.

How did he feel as he settled down in Alexander Hall on the seminary campus, unpacked his belongings, took stock of his resources, drew in a long breath, and faced the future?

"Even though I was a country boy about to knock heads with some of the great minds in America," he says, "I was confident I could hold my own. I'd been well instructed by the things I'd learned philosophically under Dr. W. H. Jellema."

> Two roads diverged. . . . , and I—
> I took the one less traveled by,
> And that has made all the difference.[2]

---

[2]*Ibid.*

CHAPTER 6
Geerhardus Vos

"An institution," Emerson said, "is the lengthened shadow of a man."

In Kees Van Til's generation, Princeton Theological Seminary was the lengthened shadow of its faculty, an assembly of scholars of the highest caliber. Of the men on that distinguished staff, none exercised more influence on the young man from the fields of Indiana than Dr. Geerhardus Vos.

There could be a natural reason for this. Both teacher and student had had their roots in the soil of the Netherlands. Both were subjects of godly upbringing. Both had been associated with the stalwart *Afecheiding.* Both had studied at Calvin and Princeton. Both (projecting Van Til into the future) taught at Princeton.

Yet the cement that held the two together in a kind of Paul-Timothy relationship went beyond the things they had in common. Geerhardus was an intellectual colossus. On the strength of a fellowship, he had been enabled to take post-graduate work in Berlin and Strassbourg (at approximately the same time Albert Schweitzer was studying there). His dissertation on certain texts of the

Assyrian language attracted the attention of linguists all over the Continent. The lecture notes he jotted down while teaching systematic theology at Calvin Seminary are a priceless treasure. A scholar who has been fortunate enough to read them says: "They constitute one of the still untapped gold mines of biblical doctrine." His *Biblical Theology, Self-Disclosure of Jesus,* and *Structure of Pauline Eschatology,* representing massive scholarship, catapulted him into international prominence. He contributed regularly to the *Princeton Theological Review.*

Quite naturally, the range and depth of his learning had the effect of animating the latent powers stirring in the brain of seminarian Van Til.

Another dimension to the older man that left an even more lasting impression on the younger was his walk with the Lord. Van Til could have said of him what the Shunammite said of Elijah: "This is an holy man of God which passeth by us continually" (2 Kings 4:9). His piety was not the kind worn on the sleeve. It was, rather, unpretentious, unexhibited, like ocean currents flowing in the cavernous deep.

Some of the versatility of the theologian shines forth in two books he penned in his leisure hours: *Charis* (1931) and *Western Rhymes* (1933), which contained the best of his poems.

He must have been proud of his family. His wife, Catherine, wrote a marvelous volume, *Children's Story Bible,* which has been a real boon not only to little ones, but to adults as well. One of his four sons, Johannes, served as a missionary to Manchuria, China, and later taught Bible courses at Geneva College. The other children have also performed yeoman service in God's kingdom.

In the sunset of his life, Dr. Vos viewed with considerable uneasiness the progress of a struggle going on in the Presbyterian Church, U.S.A. For years the liberals, not satisfied with having taken over every other divinity school operating under the supervision of its General Assembly, were working feverishly to gain control of Princeton, the last outpost of Reformed theology. They had managed to jockey Dr. J. Ross Stevenson, a professing conservative but a practicing "middle-of-the-roader," into the office of president. Stevenson's goal was to make the seminary a marketplace for every shade of doctrine being propagated in the whole church, not just the solidly Calvinistic truths Princeton had taught since its founding.

It seems clear now that Geerhardus Vos knew that Van Til, with his vast potential for getting at the heart of issues and defining and defending the truth, would be an effective combatant in the struggle. In good Paul-to-Timothy fashion, the venerable Vos exhorted the budding philosopher-theologian to prepare to fight the good fight of faith.

He knew very well that Kees was reticent about being drawn into the controversy. Kees was a member of the Christian Reformed Church and not a Presbyterian. Too, while holding iron-clad convictions, there lurked in the student an innate, ingrained strain of shyness. Moreover, Dr. Vos realized that it was Van Til's earnest desire to

minister the gospel in a rural community, away
from the developing Presbyterian crisis.

Van Til reasoned, "Why should I, an outsider,
get mixed up in a denominational skirmish when
I'm not in the denomination?"

The good professor, beginning to grow enfee-
bled by age but yet owning a warrior's heart, had,
as Van Til remembers, a ready answer: "Look, this
is going to be a much broader matter than a single
denominational issue. Princeton may be a Presbyterian seminary under the direction of the General
Assembly, but don't forget that it's a rallying point
for many, many wonderful Christian people all
over the world—people who love Reformed doctrine and life. For years it's been used by God as a
breakwater against the tides of unbelief and a
sounding board for the faith of our fathers. You
cannot, you dare not, stand by and look on like an
indifferent spectator when a conflict is being
fought in the arena."

The Voses always spent their vacations in a small
village, Roaring Branch, near Williamsport, Pennsylvania. In the summer of 1949, death lay down
with the quiet man of the Princeton Theological
Seminary faculty.

There could be no more significant commentary
on his friendship with Cornelius Van Til than that
the Vos family requested Kees to officiate at the
funeral service. He chose for his text the words of
Paul: "We know that if our earthly house of this
tabernacle were dissolved, we have a building of
God, an house not made with hands, eternal in the
heavens" (2 Cor. 5:1).

Today, under a spreading fir tree in northern Pennsylvania, there rises a simple mound of earth marking the great scholar's grave. His colleagues and students still remember him affectionately as the self-effacing man with the gaunt figure, sly wit, funny Dutch accent, fantastic grasp of the subjects he taught; the walker who was often seen perambulating the streets of Princeton accompanied by his beloved dog, Teddy.

CHAPTER 7
J. Gresham Machen

No student of the early 1920s appreciated the expertise of the Princeton Seminary pedagogues more than Kees Van Til. The formal courses in systematic theology, Old and New Testament, church history, and the electives thrilled him.

An outstanding feature of Princeton was its magnificent library, inferior to no seminary library in the nation, if indeed the world. What exhilarating, exciting hours Kees passed in the quiet booths as his mind absorbed the collected wisdom of the ages! Particularly did he revel in the nuggets he dug from the back numbers of the *Princeton Theological Review*, articles and book reviews so polished, so thorough, so stimulating they seemed to expand his mind. Often he would leave the building feeling as though he had emerged from a mental cold shower.

Another phase of seminary life he enjoyed was the social aspect. There were four eating clubs on or near the campus where the students took their meals, forged friendships, engaged in heated theological debates, and exchanged lots of good-natured banter.

Then there were the Machen "tightwad parties."
Van Til never actually had classes with J. Gresham
Machen, the erudite New Testament scholar, for he
had taken duplicate courses at Calvin. The two men
had lodging on the fourth floor of staid old Alexander Hall, Machen in a bachelor apartment, Van Til
with his friend John De Waard, who later developed into a splendid preacher. Sometimes on a
Friday or Saturday evening when Machen happened to be free from engagements, he would
throw open his door and bellow, "Don't be tightwads, boys! Don't be tightwads!"

It was his unusual signal to "come and get it."
The "it" consisted of a generous supply of fresh
fruits, nuts, cakes, cookies, candy, and iced soft-
drinks. Presumably, the "Don't be tightwads,"
meant "Don't hold back!" Machen—the boys called
him Das, a name derived from the German article in
the phrase *Das Madchen*—sat behind a checker-
board like the Autocrat of the Breakfast Table, and
invited any and all to try to beat him. He was
known to be an uncommonly skillful strategist at
the game. One by one, he would cut down his
opponents swiftly, mercilessly, and with obvious
pleasure. Kees and other thoughtful seminarians
drew an interesting parallel between the way he
overpowered his challengers at checkers and the
way he would take on scholars who openly dis-
credited the authority of the Bible, and coolly destroy their positions. His tremendous work, *The
Origin of Paul's Religion*, very well illustrated his
methodology.

John Gresham Machen, one of the four personalities who exerted the most influence on Cornelius Van Til (the others: Gerhardus Vos, Abraham Kuyper, and Klaus Schilder) was born in Baltimore, Maryland, in 1881, the son of a wealthy attorney. The Machen family sprang from English stock. Their ancestry can be traced to colonial Virginia. They were Southern Presbyterians, socially prominent, and highly regarded by the upper middle class. Machen was the son of the privileged; his options were open; he had no need of income, work, or profession. He was destined, as was his whole social class, to genteel pursuits: literature, law, science, scholarship.

Gresham attended a private academy and early showed evidence of possessing rare intellectual powers. He attended Johns Hopkins University, where he drew high praise from one of America's greatest classicists, Dr. Basil L. Gildersleeve. Upon graduating, he entered Princeton Seminary and once more his superiors saw in him rare capabilities. (It was while a seminary student that he was an occasional guest at the home of Woodrow Wilson, then president of Princeton University and a friend of the Machen family.) He went on to divinity schools in Germany and enjoyed long leisurely summers traveling through Europe. There it was that he was exposed to scintillating but destructive biblical criticism. In a sense this turned out to be a proving ground for his faith. There were periods when the testing tore his soul apart. He came through, however, strong in his confidence in the absolute trustworthiness of the Bible. The bittersweet experience invested him with a sincere sympathy for people who, like the disciple Thomas, were afflicted with intellectual perplexities. This compassion, for example, comes through in his *Christianity and Liberalism,* and *What is Faith?* Both books have proven of enormous help to college students.

In 1906, Machen joined the faculty of Princeton Seminary. Here he taught for twenty-three years, except for a tour of duty with the YMCA in France during World War I. During the war, seeing death and destruction first-hand, Machen, along with many of his contemporaries of the upper class, lost the idealism that had flourished in the United States after the Civil War.

In addition to his classroom instruction, Machen was able to turn out vitally important contributions to theological thought. In *The Origin of Paul's Religion* he devastated the thrust of German liberals who tried to drive a wedge between the teaching of Jesus and Paul. *The Virgin Birth of Christ* was hailed as the most scholarly, exhaustive, and masterful exposition and defense of that cardinal doctrine ever developed in the history of the church.

Machen's affection for his students, his kaleidescopic interests and abilities, including his infectious stratum of humor, found a compelling response in the hearts of Van Til, De Waard, and many other seminarians. One cannot converse with Cornelius Van Til for any length of time before hearing him quote Machen. "As Dassie used to say . . . ." is a favorite phrase on his lips.

If the personal integrity of Geerhardus Vos stamped its imprint on the soul of Kees Van Til, some of J. Gresham Machen's Daniel-like courage left its impact on his attitudes and outlook.

Machen was a controversial figure, not because he wanted that role, but because he nursed a compulsive, almost fierce passion to see the lordship of Christ recognized and exercised in His church. The haunting expression: "Jealous for the Crown rights of King Jesus," commonly used to describe the yearning in the breasts of the Scottish reformers, might likewise be attributed to Machen. Unless one understood this he would never be able to comprehend the man's moods or his moves. Some of his friends and acquaintances who failed to understand him urged him to stick to his teaching and stay out of controversy. He would have loved to follow their advice. The problem was, Machen looked out over the horizon and witnessed a frontal assault on the person and work of his Lord. Of course he would have loved to take a place in the eye of the storm and let others battle the elements. But to him that was tantamount to moral cowardice. A burning drive within sent him into the arena with the prescribed weapons from the armory of the King. Those he wielded with all the ardor of his aroused soul.

Machen paid a heavy price. A few faculty members and a cross-section of the student body resented his uncompromising stance. He was charged with harboring an intolerant spirit. He was a troublemaker, a heresy hunter, a "nit-picker." A whispering campaign that picked up momentum spread the word that the Machen family had made its money in the liquor business and J. Gresham became known as a "beer baron." It was a heartless, vicious lie, completely without foundation.

He bore the reproaches of Christ like the trooper he was. "I'm in good company," he would tell his friends with a sad smile. "Paul carried on his ministry with evil report and good report. The Pharisees said that our Savior was beside Himself—out of His mind. Why should men who stand for His truth not expect criticism?"

All this was not lost on young Van Til. He was beginning to see the prediction of Dr. Vos materialize. In his heart, he knew Vos was right. He knew that Machen was right. Just how or when the details of the forthcoming encounter between the forces involved were going to work out he could not tell. "One thing I want to be sure of," he would say to himself, "that when the chips are down and the going gets rough, I want God to give me the courage of Machen to do what I often sing in chapel services: Where duty calls, or danger, be never wanting there."

CHAPTER 8
Belief Is Belief and Unbelief Is Unbelief

Although Cornelius Van Til appreciated the superb quality of the teaching at Princeton Seminary, he discerned what he felt was an Achilles heel. That was the department of apologetic theology.

The courses in apologetics taught on the campus had been introduced by William Brenton Greene, Jr., in 1892. His lectures were so locked in that he had the outlines printed and distributed for convenience to the students. On the opening page of the junior class syllabus was his definition of the subject: "Apologetics—that branch of theological science setting forth to human reason the proofs that Christianity is the supernatural and exclusive religion." When Dr. Greene retired, Professor George Johnson continued to use the same program and the same approach.

The enemies of the Christian faith, in their own clever way, frequently illustrate the words of Jesus: ". . . the children of this world are in their generation wiser than the children of light" (Luke 16:8). The very philosophers the Princetonians wished refuted were the universal idealists of the era. (The idealist regards the mind as the ultimate and final reality and ideas as the objects of perception.) Theological idealists, of which school the learned Adolph Von Harnock stood out as Germany's leading spokesman, taught the universal fatherhood of God and brotherhood of man. Philosophically, the Princeton apologists offered the same weak defense against the idealists that Roman Catholic scholars Anselm and Aquinas had worked out.

The first series of arguments ran like this: It is possible to set forth reasonable proofs of the existence of God. Since an actual entity is always more real, is larger and better than one's idea of it, does it not follow that if you have an idea of something, then there has got to be an actual thing that is real and therefore more complete than the mere idea? Illustration: A glass of tea is certainly more definite and complete, more real, better in every way, than the mere idea of it. There is no way in the world you can take the *idea* of it as expressed tangibly, and drink the *idea* to quench your thirst on a hot, humid day. Application: If you posit an idea of God, logically the reality behind the idea must be more real, more complete, larger, and better than the idea. Conclusion: It is inescapable that there must be a God, otherwise people would not imperfectly conceive of one.

Dr. Greene borrowed a second set of arguments from Joseph Butler's *Analogy,* a seventeenth-century volume, widely read until recently in most English-speaking countries. Butler sought to draw analogies between common human experiences and examples found in Scripture. Christ's sacrificial sufferings, he reasoned, could be compared to a mother animal fighting to the death to protect her young.

Van Til ferreted out the flaws in these reasoning processes. The arguments, he believed, were so accommodated to human reason as to be made palatable to the sinner. On Butler's drawing board, the truths of the Word of God, including the very being of God, may be brought before the tribunal of men dead in trespasses and sins and there judged. He overlooked the fact that a cardinal tenet in the Bible is that only the regenerated heart will respond to the free offer of the gospel and rest on God's promises, that no amount of accommodating argumentation can force a rebellious human being to bow before the authority of almighty God. "The natural man receiveth not the things of the Spirit . . ." (1 Cor. 2:14). "The carnal mind is enmity against God: for it is not subject to the law of God, neither indeed can be" (Rom. 8:7). ". . . when we were enemies, we were reconciled to God by the death of his Son . . ." (Rom. 5:10).

The apologetics of Butler had originally been directed against the rationalism that flooded Europe from the close of the seventeenth century to the beginning of the nineteenth century. His method was sincere but simple. He attempted to out-rationalize the rationalists, to out-idealize the idealists. In so doing, he unwittingly accepted two of his opponents' most basic and autonomous assumptions: the thorough self-sufficiency of human reasoning and the absolute necessity of the law of contradiction. Even B. B. Warfield, reverent and

gifted scholar that he was, and in fact most evangelicals in America, never did perceive the discrepan-
cies between Butler's formulations and biblical
foundations of truth.

Another problem was coming more and more
into view. The rosy, idealistic, universal rationalism so popular in Germany had passed into
oblivion in light of the hideous carnage of World
War I trench warfare. The newer, somber mood
found comfort in the brooding existentialism of
Kierkegaard and the insane speculations of
Nietzsche. This was pure irrationalism, soon to
bury the "noble" arguments of the past.

Van Til was convinced that the point of view
presented by Abraham Kuyper in his *Encyclopedia
of Sacred Theology, Volume II,* must be the basis for a
truly biblical apologetic. Kuyper placed on the
launching pad of all thinking an antithesis between
the mind of the regenerate and the mind of the
unregenerate. Only a consistently Christian life-
and-world view, he maintained, could offer any
solution to the problem. His perceptive *Stone Lectures,* delivered at Princeton in 1898, were prepared
on the backdrop of his own observation of the history of unbelief. He could see the awesome tensions of revolution, anarchism, and humanism taking form. He envisioned the thunderheads of irrationalism about to pour drenching rains on
Europe. Nothing but a staunch biblical theism
would survive, he predicted.

He nailed down his point in the following para-
graph:

The leading thoughts that had their rise in the French Revolution at the close of the last [the eighteenth] century and in German philosophy in the course of the present [the nineteenth century], form together a life-system which is diametrically opposed to that of our fathers. Their struggles were for the sake of the glory of God and a purified Christianity; the present movement wages war for the sake of the glory of man, being inspired, not by the humble mind of Golgotha but by the pride of hero worship. And why did we, Christians, stand so weak in the face of this Modernism? Why did we constantly lose ground? Simply because we were devoid of an equal unity of life-conception, such as alone could enable us with irresistible energy to repel the enemy at the frontier. This unity of life-conception, however, is never to be found in a vague conception of Protestantism winding itself as it does in all kinds of tortuosities, but you do find it in that mighty historical process, which as Calvinism, dug a channel of its own for a more powerful stream of life.[1]

There was an even more fundamental strain running through Kuyper's *Stone Lectures* and in his other writings that ignited a spark in Van Til's thinking, that caused him to reflect on the necessity of a new approach in Christian apologetics. It was the quite startling proposition that none of the

---

[1]Abraham Kuyper, *Calvinism* (Amsterdam, 1899), p. 15ff.

areas of human life—not religion, not politics, not science, not art, not mathematics, not the uncertain future—could be understood *in the same way* by the Christian and the non-Christian. There is, he saw, a total antithesis between the mind of the saved and the mind of the lost; between the children of God and the children of the devil; between the seed of the woman and the seed of the serpent. This brings the inquirer right to the vestibule of Van Til's apologetic position.

To guard against misunderstanding, it ought to be explained that when he says in no uncertain terms, "There is no common ground," he means this: metaphysically, all human beings, as God's offspring, share the same sort of being, of course. We, whether Christian, Buddhist, Moslem, or atheist, all breathe, hunger, thirst, laugh, weep, sleep, wake, die. Epistemologically, however, the Christian and the non-Christian are not on the same wavelength. That is, they do not share the same validity of knowledge. Paul's words, "But we have the mind of Christ" (1 Cor. 2:16) is, by strong implication, exclusive as well as inclusive. The theist, the one whose eyes have been opened, looks at the western horizon as the winter sun drops out of view in an incandescent blaze of color and says, "What a great Creator to paint such a beautiful scene!" The blind man looks at the sunset and says, "Where is it?"

That is what Van Til means by epistemological antithesis. Belief is belief and unbelief is unbelief and never the twain shall meet except at the foot of the Cross.

Off the coast of Monterey Peninsula in northern California there is a spot in the Pacific where two ocean currents moving in different directions conjoin. Outwardly, no sign of a turmoil is visible. The action is altogether subsurface.

When Van Til anchored in Princeton he never dreamed he might some day become the catalyst of a new tack in Christian apologetics—at least in America. But gradually, as he read, studied, listened, discussed, pondered, and prayed two currents converged inside him: a profound, progressive love for the Reformed faith as it was taught in the seminary classrooms, and a growing unrest because he realized David was trying to fight the Lord's battle clad in Saul's armor. It grieved and saddened him.

He said nothing. He said nothing because he considered himself an outsider. He was a guest in a friendly home. It would, in his view, represent just plain bad taste to become a critic. He said nothing because he was, temperamentally, a cautious man. He said nothing because he knew there was much to be observed, much to be tasted, much to be masticated, much to be digested, and much to be assimilated before he would venture forth with a menu that at the time seemed so daring it shocked Cornelius Van Til himself.

Van Til received his Th.M. from Princeton Theological Seminary in the spring of 1925 and on September 15 married Rena Klooster. They set up housekeeping in Princeton, New Jersey. Van Til had done very well in his career both at the seminary and the university. He had won a prize as a

middler, second year student, with a paper entitled: "Evil and Theodicy" and came to the notice of
his professors as a young man highly gifted in the
area of philosophy and metaphysics. The student
body held the opinion that the Dutch students were
superior to the usual run of American college
graduates. They more or less expected the Dutch
students to walk off with the prizes, and they were
not often disappointed.

As a seminary senior Van Til wrote another
prize-winning paper, "The Will in Its Theological
Relations." His prize as a middler had been $75; his
prize as a senior was $700.

He worked his way through the undergraduate
program as a waiter and later manager of the dining
club. His advisor for his master's program in theology was the noted systematic theologian, Caspar
Wistar Hodge, one of the family of famous Hodges
who dominated Princeton's systematics for a century.

While Van Til deeply admired Machen and sided
with him in his strong and analytical opposition to
liberalism, he also had deep-seated fears about
some of the students who rallied to Machen's cause.
Van Til saw some of them as rabid reactionaries
whose actions and inflammatory speech went
against Van Til's natural tendency to be moderate
and gentle while approaching his adversaries.
Again, he was considered a "middle of the roader"
by some of his fellow students. Their criticism hurt
him, and he wondered why they did not understand his milder, but none the less persistent, resistance to the changes within the seminary.

Van Til was also taking courses each semester in the department of philosophy. His major professor was the Scottish idealist, Archibald Allan Bowman. On one occasion, Van Til wrote a thirty-nine-page paper on Hegel, drawn largely from what he already knew about the man. This very much impressed Bowman. The professor told Van Til he had a real gift for metaphysics. Apparently this judgment was passed on to Machen and others of the seminary faculty who began to speak to Van Til in terms of a teaching career. However, as he completed his examinations and dissertation for the doctorate, Van Til wanted nothing more than to be a pastor in one of the rural parishes of the Christian Reformed Church.

Cornelius and Rena Van Til were headed for a call to such a rural church in the farmlands of Michigan or Indiana, and in their minds nothing would turn them aside. But the farmer turned scholar had a burden that was beginning to bear down more heavily than ever upon him: his incredible ability to bring the claims of God's Word into the abstract world of metaphysics where few believing scholars had ventured to tread.

CHAPTER 9
A Homecoming

In June, 1927, Kees Van Til, fortified with his Th.M. and his Ph.D., was received into the Classis of Muskegon, Michigan, with plans to enter the ministry in the Christian Reformed Church. The denomination has a rule that a candidate must wait six weeks before the classis (presbytery) will process a call to a particular congregation.

Van Til decided that in the interim it would be good to make his first trip to the Netherlands since leaving that country. So, with pleasant memories of the past and dreams of the future running through his head, he turned his face toward his native land, humming:

> How dear to my heart
> Are the scenes of my childhood
> When fond recollection
> Presents them to view. . . .

At Groningen, he joined a regiment of relatives and an army of friends and acquaintances. It is a well-known fact that Hollanders are a clannish people. Because of the geographical limitations of their homeland as well as their close-knit cultural ties, they do enjoy wining and dining together, jesting, poking fun at the Dutch—"Our only virtue is stubbornness," they say of themselves—arguing, reminiscing, and genuinely rejoicing in reunions.

One of the first things Kees did in his old hometown was to look up the cobbler who had made his heavy *klompa*. What did he learn? The skillful shoemaker had packed his tools and taken off for Munster, Indiana!

Cornelius was especially interested in revisiting the large house near Enumatil, where he had passed seven of his childhood years. The graceful willow trees were there swaying in the breeze, and, to his surprise, the same sandbox was still under it. Standing there in the shade, he relived some of the happy hours he had spent playing out-of-doors.

Unexpectedly, he received a telegram from the clerk of his classis informing him that the Bates Street Christian Reformed Church in Grand Rapids had issued a call to him to be its minister. He declined, feeling that he was not ready to accept a city pastorate.

He continued his pilgrimage, returning to his birthplace at Grootegast and to De Leek, the last home of the Van Tils before they had emigrated to the States.

Another wire came to him from his classis. This communication advised him that the congregation of the Christian Reformed Church of Spring Lake, Michigan, had voted to call him to minister there. He decided that this, a small rural church, was exactly the situation he was fitted for. He sent word back that he would come.

In the fascinating city of Amsterdam, he ran into a neighbor from Highland, Indiana, Mr. Bartel Zandstra. They decided to spend a week together traveling through Germany.

Dr. Van Til often laughs when he recalls riding third and fourth class on German trains. Posted over the entrances to the tiny rooms—cubicles, actually—were the totally serious but otherwise ridiculous occupancy statements: *Sieben standplatz und Elf sitzplatz*—"seven standing room and eleven sitting room." For a pair of six-feet-tall sons of the Netherlands, this was irony stretched to the breaking point.

They also journeyed to Leipzig and inspected the famous university. Bookstores abound in that city. One can picture Van Til, with his voracious appetite for learning, browsing, scanning, reading, and wishing he had a million German marks and a dozen ships to transport tons of the theological and philosophical tomes he lovingly fingered.

In Berlin, they rode tour buses, viewed the Brandenburg Gate, and visited an armory where they watched cavalrymen go swirling by them, brandishing metal cuirasses. They also invaded the ornate Kaiser Palace at Potsdam. Van Til still remembers the fabulous drawing room decorated with stones gathered from all over the earth. The sight of the world-famous chandelier, displaying its brilliant crystals, continues to linger in his mind. He has used it as an illustration of the glory and majesty of God when the redeemed will stand before the throne and see the King in his beauty: when they will be "lost in wonder, love, and praise."

Before taking their leave of Berlin, the visitors walked down the *Siegesalle-Unter den Linden,* the Victory Boulevard under the Linden Trees. On that identical spot, Adolf Hitler would soon stand and furiously pound out platitudes before his screaming, worshiping supporters.

They passed their last day in Germany sightseeing in bustling Hamburg. Van Til chuckles as he says that it is the custom for the waiters in restaurants in Hamburg not to ask whether or not you want beer but to simply ask what kind, light or dark? "No self-respecting waiter would deal just with the *genus* but only with the *species,*" he says, philosophically. "He must know the particular kind. Surely, I thought, I must try *dunkles* before leaving Deutschland and returning to Groningen and the warm-hearted reception of my relatives. You may guess as much as you wish; I shall remain forever silent. I am resolute in my conviction that I shall never, no never, order *dunkles* again."

Before saying goodbye to his fatherland, Kees made contacts with scholars like Herman Riddebos and G. C. Berkouwer, both coming to be recognized at home and abroad as outstanding teachers and writers. He also was invited to take part in a wedding conducted by a Hungarian Reformed clergyman. He offered appropriate remarks, which were translated from Dutch to the Hungarian language.

After that it was back to America and his beloved

wife, to Spring Lake, and into his first, and only, pastorate. He returned rested, invigorated, and eager to begin work.

The Van Tils loved their life at Spring Lake with the rural congregation of seventy Dutch families. They fully expected to stay there for several years. But it was not to be. In the summer of 1928, Van Til received an offer to teach apologetics at his alma mater. He took a leave of absence from his pastoral duties, and he and Rena headed for Princeton.

CHAPTER 10

The Presuppositional Approach

It would be a mistake to imply that Cornelius Van Til did not enjoy teaching. Just as he was at ease in the pulpit, he was equally relaxed on the platform facing his classes. From the start of his pedagogical labors he was able to establish an excellent rapport with his students. There is no question that he enjoyed the image of professorship and the respect of young seminarians.

The study of apologetics is by no means a simple discipline. The subject, being abstract, is considerably more difficult to put across than, say, church history, which deals with the concrete. Dr. Van Til's disarmingly innocent manner, his use of the blackboard and chalk, the delightful way he would weave humor into his lectures, and his patience with impatient students won the affection of all. That was true even of young seminarians who did not agree with him. Sometimes these would come away from his class knitting their brows and shaking their heads and saying, "We just can't swallow what he's been dishing out, but we have to say there isn't anything upstage about the man."

His appointment to the department of apolo-

getics meant the end of the William Brenton Greene
approach to truth, and the commencement of what
has been called the "presuppositional" method,
based on Abraham Kuyper's work; better, it was
based on the Bible. It is Van Til's contention that
nowhere do the Scriptures seek to establish the
existence of God or the verities of the gospel of
Christ by human reason. Scripture presupposes
God's existence. "In the beginning God created the
heaven and the earth" (Gen. 1:1). ". . . he that
cometh to God must believe that he is, and that he
is a rewarder of them that diligently seek him"
(Heb. 11:6). ". . . Christ died for our sins *according
to the scriptures*" (1 Cor. 15:3, italics ours).

In his study, Van Til dealt specifically with the
Hegelian ideas found in the works of Hegel's
British followers, Francis Herbert Bradley and Bernard Bosanquet. Van Til demonstrated conclu-
sively that the God of idealism was not the God of
Scripture and that ultimately absolutism faded into
pragmatism, its avowed enemy. The relationship
between God and man based on idealism was not
one of Creator to creature nor of sinner to Redeemer
but one of a metaphysical nature in which there is
no distinct difference between God and man.

There was something else Van Til discovered in
his careful analysis of the post-Kantian metaphysi-
cians: their insight into the necessity of presuppositions. They recognized that the given presuppositions of any philosophical position predetermined
and governed much of its later outworkings. This
notion led Van Til to the realization that while the
apologetic of Joseph Butler was orthodox in its in-

tent, it failed in that it did not criticize the unbelieving presuppositions of its adversaries but, in fact, accepted those very presuppositions. The notion of the presupposition was not wrong; rather it was its non-Christian content that led to centuries of error in apologetics. Van Til thus introduced his basic notion in apologetics, his pioneering insight, that the presuppositions and not merely the attendant argument have to be thoroughly Christian, that is, scriptural.

Van Til's summation and penetrating criticism of the work of an intellectual giant like Alfred North Whitehead demonstrated that even in his first year of teaching, at age thirty-two, he had developed a thoroughly biblical standard against which humanistic, unbelieving philosophies could be judged. In his first article in the *Princeton Theological Review* he wrote:

> We have then in Whitehead's thinking what we find in much of modern philosophy, namely, an ambiguity in the conception of God. In so far as He is conceived to be transcendent He may be personal but is finite; in so far as He is immanent He becomes the depersonalized universal realised in the historic particulars. Among the idealistic thinkers this ambiguity is so persistent and so carefully concealed that at one time the Absolute or God is portrayed as a Moloch who devours both space and time, reducing all our experience to "appearances"; while at another time He is represented as needing the space-time world, and

being subject to its conditions. More realistic thinkers such as Dr. Whitehead, who hate all acosmism, cannot consistently hold that God is a "non-temporal actual entity." The logic of their position must bring down the transcendent God till He becomes a "function" in the world, an "element" in life. "He is the binding element in the world" (p. 158).

For Theism it is important that God be not thus conceived as a universal realising Himself in historic particulars; Theism's God is the self-sufficient creator of the "epochal occasions," or historic particulars. Our conclusion is that Dr. Whitehead's thought displays a strongly antitheistic tendency. When he made time and change a necessary aspect of all reality he gave possibility an independent metaphysical status; God could be no more than an aspect, an "element" or a "function" in reality as a whole. Theism makes God the source of possibility; only thus can the transcendence as well as the immanence of God be maintained; only thus is God qualitatively distinct from man; only thus is He personal; only thus is He God.[1]

It is somewhat surprising that the new apologetic did not cause a great deal of stir in the Christian community. There were probably two reasons: (1) the implications of the position did not register for some time to come, and (2), Princeton Seminary

---

[1] *Princeton Theological Review*, vol. 27 (1929), p. 135ff.

was seething with unrest over what looked definitely like a change in its administration, with far-reaching doctrinal consequences.

Cornelius went about his duties quietly and sensibly, avoiding the sensational and the spectacular.

In spite of his busy routine, he took time to write a double review of two books by Holland's foremost systematic theologian, Herman Bavinck. The books, titled *Paedagogische Beguiselen* and *De Nieuwe Opvoeding,* defined Bavinck's educational methodology. The reviews were run in the last issue of the *Princeton Theological Review*. That remarkable journal was discontinued, significantly and tragically, at the time of the disruption that took place in 1929.

His treatment of Bavinck's material demonstrated Van Til's system of thought, namely, that no aspect of life or of society is neutral—a demilitarized zone, if you will. Every aspect of life or society is either pro-Christian or anti-Christian, just as surely as Christ's assertion, "He that is not for me is against me" (Matt. 12:30), is a proposition that slices away all neutrality.

Van Til also enthusiastically endorsed Bavinck's analysis of secular education. Said Bavinck:

Law is but a man-made ideal possessing no section that may be called divine; expediency displaces authority, while the sacred and the secular are merged into one. As to the goal of education, modern pedagogy frankly asserts that it is man. Man being already autonomous in philosophy, in religion, in art and even in morality, it remains only that the autonomy be recognized the moment you see him in the cradle. Let the child, the babe, even, proceed to educate himself.[2]

All of which points up the need for the establishment of Christian schools, Dr. Bavinck concludes, to counteract the deadly effect of the poison of humanism and for the equipping of Christian youth for kingdom service. Nobody endorses the point more enthusiastically than Van Til. It is a logical corollary of his whole apologetic system.

The school year 1928–29 passed undramatically for the Van Tils. They enjoyed many features of their new life. There is always something exhilarating about contacts with young people. They appreciated the fellowship with many of those of like precious faith, certain members of the faculty and returning alumni. They took advantage of the cultural programs presented on the university campus. They liked to walk through the quiet streets of Princeton. They found their association with J. Gresham Machen to be an especially enriching and rewarding relationship.

Then, too, Cornelius would have been less than human had he not derived a certain legitimate gratification from the prestige of serving with a corps of distinguished scholars such as those teaching on the Princeton Seminary staff. He was the youngest member of the faculty. The quality of his work was being observed and approved by the men

[2]*Ibid.*

on the board of directors. Their approval was made evident in the spring of 1929 when the board offered him the Chair of Apologetics, the equivalent of a full professorship—a flattering gesture, indeed.

Meanwhile, events were moving rapidly toward a crisis on the campus. That crisis was to bring Dr. Van Til inexorably to a point in his career where he would be forced to stand once more at the crossroads, a place that by now must have had all the overtones of familiarity.

CHAPTER 11

Westminster Theological Seminary

For many years the administration of Princeton Seminary had been regulated by two organizations: the Board of Directors and the Board of Trustees. The Board of Directors supervised the program of education. The Board of Trustees held title deed to the property but had nothing to do with the educational program. Those serving as directors, men of integrity and conviction, had seen to it that the seminary had remained unswervingly faithful to its biblical commitment in accordance with its charter.

The first sign of trouble came in the form of a student protest, which surfaced in February, 1909. A large number of first-year students signed a petition stating that a more "practical" approach to the ministry, rather than the purely intellectual and scholastic themes to which they were subject, would be preferred. The Board stuck by the faculty and nothing was changed.

The really basic issue, however, smoldered on for some years, but finally burst into a new confrontation in 1914 on the very eve of the First World War.

The issue was the selection of a successor to the president, Dr. Francis L. Patton.

Patton had been with the seminary since 1902. He had served the office in a humble manner, allowing the faculty to make decisions with him. At an anniversary celebration of the seminary held in 1912, Patton stated in no uncertain terms the conservative nature of his image of the seminary:

> Now Princeton Seminary, it should be said, never contributed anything to these modifications of the Calvinist system. She went on defending the traditions of the Reformed theology. You may say that she was not original: perhaps so, but then, neither was she provincial. She had no oddities of manner, no shibboleths, no pet phrases, no theological labels, no trademark. She simply taught the old Calvinistic theology without modification: and she made obstinate resistance to the modifications proposed elsewhere, as being in their logical results subversive of the Reformed faith. There has been a New Haven theology and an Andover theology; but there never was a distinctly Princeton theology.

However, by 1914 the liberally minded church leaders, unhappy with what they considered a narrow and crabbed Calvinism, decided it was time for a change. Their ultimate weapon was a man.

The manipulators were careful not to have a modernist installed in the office of president. That would have been too revolutionary. They needed a churchman who would profess his orthodoxy but at the same time be tolerant toward every wind of doctrine blowing across the church. Their ideal representative was Dr. J. Ross Stevenson, a minister whose ideas of theological education, Machen said, "were ruinous." Stevenson constantly orchestrated his evangelicalism but, with his colleague, Dr. Charles Erdman, was never known to take a public stand against what Walter Lippmann called "the acids of modernity." It was no secret that Stevenson's objective was to have the seminary reflect every shade of theological opinion in the denomination, not just the sturdy Reformed emphasis that had distinguished the school from its inception.

In the years following Stevenson's installment, the theologically liberal pastors and laymen within the Presbyterian Church in the U.S.A. (the northern church) continued to gain a foothold.

In 1922, the year Van Til came to Princeton Seminary as a student, Harry Emerson Fosdick preached his famous (or infamous) sermon, "Shall the Fundamentalists Win?" A Baptist minister serving as assistant pastor in the old First Presbyterian Church in New York City, Fosdick was openly challenging the conservatives within the Presbyterian Church.

The 1923 General Assembly of the Presbyterian Church voted in favor of an overture admonishing the Presbytery of New York to see that those who preach in the First Church adhere to the doctrines of the denomination. In response to this action, however, 1,300 Presbyterian clergyman signed the iniquitous doctrine known as the *Auburn Affirma-tion*. The *Affirmation* (a misnomer if there ever was one) declared that such basic doctrines as "the in-spiration of the Bible, the Incarnation, the Atone-ment, the Resurrection, and his [Christ's] continu-ing Life and Supernatural Power" were, in effect, man-formulated theories, and that they were not the only theories allowed by Scripture. Given this view, it was felt that ordination should not be de-termined by the candidates' interpretation of those doctrines.

The move toward theological liberalism within the denomination was a source of strife at Princeton as well. In 1929, at the Presbyterian General As-sembly, which met in St. Paul, the issue came to a head. A commissioner moved to do away with the seminary's two controlling boards in favor of one. Machen, one of the commissioners, rose to speak against the motion. He was generously allowed five minutes to plead his case! Eloquently and fer-vently, he appealed to the Assembly to defeat the motion. Not to do so, he warned, would signify a drastic move away from the historic faith for which Princeton had always stood. It would mean the decline and fall of a truly great institution.

The moderator put the question. By a written count of 530 to 300 the delegates voted affirma-tively. It seems unbelievable that a body of churchmen, sitting in a solemn session as a court of Jesus Christ, in less than half an hour—the total time allotted for debate—could, and did, radically alter the direction of a theological seminary originally dedicated to the task of preparing young men to proclaim the unadulterated Word of God.

The Assembly went on to legislate two more significant pieces of business. It established a Board of Trustees consisting of one third from the Board of Directors, one third from the Board of Trustees, and one third from the church at large, to have complete charge of the administration.

The Assembly proceeded to elect to the new Board of Trustees two ministers who had signed the *Auburn Affirmation*. It is not to be wondered that evangelicals left St. Paul distressed.

Promptly, four members of the Princeton Seminary faculty, Robert Dick Wilson, Oswald T. Allis, J. Gresham Machen, and Cornelius Van Til, tendered their resignations in protest against the shattering maneuvers of the General Assembly.

Van Til returned to his Spring Lake pastorate. The others turned their attention to a new endeavor.

Chiefly through the initiative of a group of staunch, discerning Presbyterian laymen, plans were started to erect a seminary to continue the witness of Princeton. The idea caught on at once. The natural site would be Philadelphia. The name would be Westminster Theological Seminary. Dr. Allis was good enough to devote to the cause a large brown stone building on Pine Street, near the center of the city. It would be adequate to meet the current needs. The students were to live in a hotel.

The first class of the new institution was to be held on September 25, 1929, with fifty students.

Many were former students from Princeton who, like the heart of that famous faculty, were now a seminary in exile.

From its beginning, Westminster was kept free from ecclesiastical control. A self-perpetuating Board of Trustees, working in close collaboration with the faculty, was to regulate the affairs, administrative and educational. There would be no president, but rather a chairman of the faculty. The choice was Machen.

In conservative Presbyterian circles all over the country enormous interest in the new development was stirring. Prominent ministers like Clarence Edward Macartney, Frank Stevenson, Charles Schall, Paul McConkey, journalist Samuel Craig, influential laymen such as Frederic M. Paist and T. Edward Ross threw their support behind the institution.

Four younger men, able but not as well-known as the Princeton professors, were added to the faculty: the Reverend R. B. Kuiper, Ned Stonehouse, Allan MacRae, and Paul Woolley. The "Magnificent Seven" made up a small but exceedingly versatile staff.

Robert Dick Wilson, approaching seventy, had mastered thirty different Semitic languages, was internationally acknowledged as an authority on the Old Testament books and linguistics, and was a relentless foe of so-called "higher criticism."

Oswald T. Allis, his running-mate in the Old Testament department, had for years edited the *Princeton Theological Review* in addition to his teaching. He had also written thought-provoking books, including *Prophecy and the Church,* a work that aroused no little controversy among the ranks of evangelicals. Everyone who ever came in contact with Dr. Allis, whether friend or foe, knew him to be a courtly, cultured Christian gentleman.

J. Gresham Machen had no peer in the field of New Testament scholarship. Gifted not only as a theologian, he had a rare ability to teach his courses in a way that made them exciting. Ironical was the fact that although he was the target of abuse and sometimes ridicule on the part of certain church leaders, philosophical humanists like Walter Lippmann and H. L. Mencken praised his worth in glowing terms. For the cause of Westminster, Machen was willing to pledge his life, his fortune, and his reputation.

Of the new men, R. B. Kuiper, who would teach homiletics, was reputed to be one of the finest pulpiteers in the nation. Dr. C. W. Hodge had heartily recommended him for the post. Coming from a Christian Reformed background and a rich experience in the preaching ministry, he promised, after much deliberation, to teach for one year.

Boyish-looking Ned Stonehouse was the selection to break in as Machen's understudy. A product of Calvin College, Princeton Seminary, and The Free University in Amsterdam, he had been singled out as a budding linguist by no less a notable than the Dutch scholar, Dr. Grosheide. Grosheide said of him, comically, "He eats up Syriac like bacon." From his first day at Westminster, Ned established an unusually fine rapport with the students. One reason: He was wild about sports.

Paul Woolley, out of Princeton University, Princeton Seminary, and Westminster College, Cambridge, would be doubling as instructor in church history and registrar. Married to Helen Von Der Pahlin, a young lady of Russian nobility, they had purposed to serve God as missionaries to China, but continuing upheavals in the Orient blocked their plans. Woolley's mind operated like a tape recorder. To this day he carries about a phenomenal amount of knowledge in that active core under his skull. He is also, incidentally, an authority on railroads.

Allan MacRae finished his post-graduate work in Berlin in time to take up his assignment in the Old Testament department. Serious, hard-working, conscientious, he was a model for the students in the matter of "redeeming the time." Unfortunately, he was not to stay long at Westminster.

It was a redoubtable unit that prepared to meet the original student body in September, 1929, "a band of men whose hearts God had touched." They had counted the cost and to a person were willing to suffer. As a matter of fact, there were times that fall when checks would come in late although the stipend was a relatively low amount. There was never any complaining.

One problem: A great gap, an all-important gap, existed in the faculty ranks. Who would teach apologetics?

All eyes turned to Cornelius Van Til.

He received an invitation to come to Philadelphia.

He was happy to be back in Spring Lake with his

beloved flock. Much as he had enjoyed his year at Princeton, he was so completely at home in the serene atmosphere of rural Michigan, able to preach, call, counsel, and comfort, that it was like a new lease on life.

He turned down the invitation. Rena, who was expecting an arrival, rejoiced.

Dr. Allis journeyed to Spring Lake to plead with Van Til to change his mind.

Van Til was adamant.

In August Machen, accompanied by Ned Stonehouse, went to visit him with a suitcase full of arguments. He was needed desperately to bridge the gap in apologetics. Who else would qualify? Think of the opportunities to help mold the thinking of many young knights of the pulpit. Think of the preferments aging Robert Dick Wilson had given up at Princeton.

Looking back, Kees Van Til will tell you, smiling, that all he could think of was the instance of William Farrel pressuring John Calvin to settle in Geneva, even though everything in Calvin militated against the thought.

He still held out. ("We aren't called stubborn Dutchmen without cause.")

Machen and Stonehouse returned to Philadelphia, utterly discouraged.

No one in the world but Rena will ever know what tensions, what conflicts, what terrible agony ripped through the sensitive soul of her husband in the weeks following the interview. Everything signaled for him to stay where he was. He was a pastor; all his life he had trained for the pastorate.

The Lord had put the seal of His approval on His servant's ministry in Spring Lake. Kees hated large cities, and Rena hated them still more. How could he possibly ask his precious spouse to give up her good life for a miserable climate in a crowded city?

There was still another questionable feature about lining up with the Westminster men. Van Til had observed, while at Princeton, that some of the students, intensely loyal to Machen and everything he represented, were loudly and disconcertingly argumentative. They did more harm to the cause than good, he often thought. It is always so with strong men involved in a great cause. It was so with Luther and with Calvin. It was so with Machen. Van Til himself, mild by disposition, never one to provoke a controversy needlessly, shied away from the type of associations he would inevitably have in Philadelphia.

His decision was final. Absolutely, irrevocably final. He would remain in Spring Lake.

Come the middle of September, 1929, a few days before Westminster Seminary was to hold its initial opening exercises in Witherspoon Hall, word came that C. Van Til would join the faculty.

CHAPTER 12
Van Til Vs. Modernism

The Van Tils, with their tiny two-and-a-half-months-old son Earl, took up residence in a house owned by Dr. Allis. The location was near the seminary.

The decision to leave their pastorate the second time was harder on the Van Tils than it had been the first time. For the family, it was another period of adjustment. Rena, in particular, found conditions hard to accept. Her husband was away from home a great deal of the time occupied with his teaching duties or out of town fulfilling preaching engagements. She became unendurably lonely. The contrast between the dust and maddening roar of Philadelphia and the clean, peaceful atmosphere of Spring Lake was startling. She was desperately homesick for the country. Added to her other trials, swarms of black ants insisted on holding conferences in her otherwise immaculate kitchen. She fought them fiercely. Just as fiercely she fought to keep from falling into the pit of despair.

For Cornelius, the change was less difficult. He was forced to keep busy with a tight work schedule. But in leisure moments his mercurial mind would stray back to his carefree boyhood days in Holland, to the green fields of the Midwest, or to the calm, relaxed climate of Princeton. He also struggled to ward off attacks of self-pity.

Still, he and Rena had made the joint decision to come to Philadelphia in the spirit of David when he said to Araunah, ". . . neither will I offer burnt offerings unto the LORD my God of that which doth cost me nothing" (2 Sam. 24:24). They trusted implicitly in a sovereign King who makes no mistakes. They were in Philadelphia according to the purpose of the One who works all things according to the counsel of His will. They determined, therefore, to submit to their lot cheerfully, and believe that the Lord in His good time would bring them through fire and water into a wealthy place.

The beginning of Westminster Theological Seminary was not dramatically auspicious. Seven faculty members and fifty students were to teach and study in a rather gloomy four-story residence in downtown Philadelphia. No powerful denomination was to subsidize the project. The nation was poised on the brink of a financial recession. Westminster was not great, as the world counts greatness. Yet pulsing through both faculty members and students was a kind of vibration, almost electric in its force. They were on lowly Pine Street representing a cause, to them a valiant cause, and like Gideon's reduced band, they thrilled to it.

At the opening exercises of the new institution, chairman of the faculty, J. Gresham Machen, stated the purpose of the seminary:

No, my friends, though Princeton Seminary is dead, the noble tradition of Princeton Seminary is alive. Westminster Seminary will endeavor by God's grace to continue that tradition unimpaired; it will endeavor, not on a foundation of equivocation and compromise, but on an honest foundation of devotion to God's Word, to maintain the same principles that Old Princeton maintained. We believe, first, that the Christian religion, as it is set forth in the Confession of Faith of the Presbyterian Church, is true; we believe, second, that the Christian religion welcomes and is capable of scholarly defense; and we believe, third, that the Christian religion should be proclaimed without fear or favor, and in clear opposition to whatever opposes it, whether within or without the church, as the only way of salvation for lost mankind.

At the new seminary, Van Til taught the same subjects and courses he had taught at Princeton. His junior apologetics class was required. For this he wrote out his notes. Gradually, the notes were expanded, refined, and distributed to the students in the form of syllabi. (He refers to them as "sillybuses" and downgrades them.) These in turn were converted into booklets. He had the words, "Not to be considered a published work," printed on the front page of the booklets. What this means he has never made clear. Certainly many generations of young men who have studied under him have treasured the material and have used it profitably in their own teaching.

Cornelius also continued to teach the elective course in the history of metaphysics. It was an outgrowth of his dissertation at Princeton University. What he attempted was a bold move. He went for Immanuel Kant's Achilles' heel.

The aim of Kant's intricate philosophical-theological system was to rescue the structure of philosophy from the tentacles of Newton's physics. Newton wanted to have physics encircle all human thought. Kant reached back to the Greeks and came up as the architect of a new system in which time was ultimate and the universe divided into two spheres: the noumenal, the realm of perfect or true knowledge of the thing-in-itself, and the phenomenal, the realm of everyday experience, which is always imperfect and even irrational. The noumenal has to do with purely intellectual intuition, the phenomenal with practical wisdom and experiential decision. In the eyes of many philosophers it appeared as though Kant had saved God from the ogre of science, and that worship could continue side-by-side with theory. In the history of philosophy, Hydra-minded Hegel followed Kant. Van Til undertook the Herculean task of tracing intelligently the formulations of Kierkegaard and of contemporary German schools of thought back to Hegel and Kant. This was the sperm out of which, in his teaching and later writings, he sought to fashion the body of his polemic.

Perhaps there is truth in the conclusion some have drawn that as Billy Sunday was considered a messenger of salvation to outcasts, to "down-and-outers," Van Til might be thought of as a missionary to people who are socially and culturally "up-and-outers." What he has tried to do is to unmask the disguises by which intellectuals have sought to falsify the content of the Christian faith and substitute human philosophy and man-made theology for God-revealed truth.

To do this he has utilized a two-pronged offensive. He has taken the true gospel, as God has given him opportunity, to all who will grant him a hearing; and he has attempted faithfully to teach his students to defend as well as define the faith once delivered to the saints.

"It is always interesting to me that so many of our fashionable ministers keep telling us, 'The gospel doesn't need defending,' " he says with flashing eyes. "So what do they do with Paul? He told the Philippians, 'I am set for the defense of the gospel.' " He chuckles. "Dassie used to remind us that preachers who insist that the gospel needs no defense usually have no gospel to defend. How true!"

A good instance of the use of his second prong comes through in one of his little books, *The Reformed Pastor and Modern Thought*. Here he spells out some of the themes of his lectures given over the years at Westminster. In simple form he describes the strains in modern thought and their effect on the Christian witness. The endeavor inevitably takes him into areas where he crosses swords with most of the leaders of modern thought.

In the early thirties, Dr. Van Til became interested in a young Swiss pastor-scholar, Karl Barth.

Barth had received instruction from Von Harnack. In the twenties, he was not well-known to American theologians. Van Til detected a dangerous trend in his theology, especially in the man's double use of language, which in fact led not a few evangelicals to accept him into the evangelical camp. His influence spread rapidly and widely. It developed into the movement sometimes called neo-orthodoxy. Van Til was not deceived. Eventually, he was to produce an important book, *The New Modernism*, which unveiled Barth's liberalism in its stark reality.

A capsulated form of Karl Barth's view of the Bible is admirably stated by Van Til in the opening chapter of *Jerusalem and Athens* entitled "My Credo":

> If non-Reformed evangelical theologies tend toward subjectivism, modern non-evangelical theology stands on it flat-footed! Take the theology of Karl Barth, for example. The free grace of God, Barth maintained, could not be communicated through a stabilized, objectivized revelation. Orthodox theology, he argues, has reduced the living, active revelation of God to that of a lifeless form. When Barth spoke agreeably, therefore, of verbal inspiration he "actualized" it and therewith fitted it "into his system." In bringing down the Bible to the dimension of "causal relations," orthodoxy brings down the entire religious relation between God and man to the level of impersonal concepts and ideas. Orthodoxy is the theology

of the "blessed possessors," the theology of those who control the freedom of God. The God of orthodoxy, indeed the God of Calvinism, is not sovereign! The God of Calvin is not the God of sovereign, universal grace.

We may say, therefore, that the Barthian soteriology of "sovereign, free grace" which comes to us only in our subjectivity entails a radically new view of Scripture itself. The Bible may now be called the Word of God only in so far as it brings this message of subjectivity to us. To say "the Bible is the Word of God," for Barth, does not imply a directly discernible revelation of God in history as we know it.

CHAPTER 13

The Presbyterian Conflict

Throughout the last hectic months at Princeton and the early segment of seminary life in Philadelphia, it is not clear how many of the Westminster men were aware of the basic and far-reaching revolution going on in the orbit of apologetics. Did Machen understand how far from the old Princeton apologetic the new Westminster apologetic really was? Did Machen realize that Van Til, R. B. Kuiper, and Ned Stonehouse had brought to Philadelphia the best of Amsterdam? Had the thought actually registered that a new direction in apologetics in America was being charted?

Van Til honestly does not know the answers. He traveled with Machen on a two-day train trip to and from Chicago (Machen was fanatically fond of railroads), during which time he tried carefully to explain his developing system. Just how much of the information filtered through to Das, with myriads of administrative and logistical problems burdening his already overworked brain, Cornelius could not tell. It is a known fact that Machen, as far as he comprehended it, fully endorsed Van Til's thinking and gave it his hearty and unqualified backing.

In the early chapters in the life of Westminster, several events of vital importance took place.

To the grief of the evangelical world, Dr. Robert Dick Wilson passed away. His monumental contribution to biblical scholarship is inestimable. The distinguishing mark of his work was thoroughness. Especially powerful was his defense of the historical accuracy of those sections of the Old Testament that had come under fire from S. R. Driver and other leading destructive critics. Dr. Wilson, for all his erudition, gave expression in simple terms to his complete confidence in both the written Word and the living Word.

In Hebrew class at Princeton, he would often stand before the students and say, "Boys, I must admit there are questions that sometimes bother me when I read the Bible. This I can understand because I'm a sinner and my understanding is limited, so I'm not going to charge God with not being clear. I'm going to lay it to my own ignorance. But I will say this: after studying God's Word for over fifty years I have come to the conclusion that no man on earth knows enough to claim there is a single inaccuracy in the original Scriptures of the Old and New Testaments."

At Westminster, his students will always remember the time when, with deep feeling, he said, "Although there is much in Scripture I do not presume to know exhaustively, one thing I am sure of and that is, I can say, in the words of the children's hymn: 'Jesus loves me, this I know, For the Bible tells me so.' "

In Systematic Theology, R. B. Kuiper left at the end of the first year after putting in nine months of marvelously lucid instruction. He was succeeded by a promising young scholar, John Murray. When Kuiper returned later, he taught homiletics.

Coming out of a richly endowed covenanter background, Murray brought to Philadelphia a delightful Scottish burr in his speech, a rare insight into Scripture, and a devotional life that had a telling impact on the lives of his students. No one who listened to his chapel prayers can ever forget the profound reverence in his approach to the divine throne, the unaffected humility of the man, and the natural way he would weave portions of the Psalter into his intercession.

There is a favorite story his protegés like to tell on him, and which he used to laugh over. In World War I, he served his country in the Black Watch Battalion, and lost an eye in combat. He had it replaced with a plastic eye. One day, the story goes, a new student said to an older student, "Somebody's done a great job manufacturing Mr. Murray's plastic eye. It's so genuine I can't tell the plastic eye from the real one. How can you tell the difference?" The older student, aware of the fact that Mr. Murray was a notoriously hard marker, said, facetiously, "I'll tell you how you can spot the difference. You want to study both eyes carefully and if you see a gleam of mercy in one, that's the plastic eye."

Murray had received his master's degree from the University of Glasgow in 1922. In 1927, he was

awarded both the Th.B. and the Th.M. degrees
from Princeton Seminary. Having received a fellowship upon graduation from Princeton, Murray
decided to apply it to further theological study in
his homeland at New College, Edinburgh.

In 1929, at the age of thirty-one, Murray returned
to Princeton to assist Caspar Wistar Hodge in teaching systematic theology. However, Murray quickly
saw that Old Princeton was gone—along with the
heart of its conservative faculty and the League of
Evangelical Students with whom he had enjoyed
fellowship during his student days. They had all
left to found Westminster Theological Seminary,
and in 1930, after his obligation to Princeton ended,
Murray joined them. Murray and Van Til, with
their strong personalities, really formed the poles
around which the world of Westminster was to turn
for over forty years.

Of the original Westminster student body only a
slight majority were, by affiliation, Presbyterians.
(It is interesting that in the first junior class approximately a dozen Methodist youths registered.) The
question then came up, where would graduates of
Presbyterian persuasion go, ecclesiastically? A few
planned to enter the ranks of the Presbyterian
Church U.S. (Southern Presbyterian). Most decided to apply for pulpits in the Presbyterian
Church, U.S.A. (Northern Presbyterian). It was to
be expected that in view of its historical background, Westminster graduates should be marked
men. In the eyes of not a few Presbyterian ministers, Machen had committed the unpardonable sin

for spearheading the rupture with Princeton. Increasingly, the truth was coming out that many liberals were anything but liberal in their conduct.

Two years after Westminster's break with Princeton, there arose on the ecclesiastical horizon a cloud no larger than a man's hand. Probably at the time few foresaw that the cloud would take on the proportions of a thunderhead and affect the lives of multitudes of people.

Two elements combined to create the formation of the cloud.

A group of Protestant laymen known as the Appraisal Commission, with liberal Dr. William Ernest Hocking of Harvard University acting as its chairman, visited various mission stations overseas, returned to America, and put together a book, *Rethinking Missions*, which as it turned out, contained a sizzling fuse.

In his five-page review of the book, Dr. Machen said:

It deprecates the distinction between Christians and non-Christians; it belittles the Bible and inveighs against Christian doctrine; it dismisses the doctrine of eternal punishment as a doctrine antiquated even in Christendom; it presents Jesus as a religious Teacher and Example, as Christianity's "highest expression of the religious life," but certainly not as very God of very God; it belittles evangelism, definite conversions, very open profession of faith in Christ, membership in the Christian Church, and substitutes the "dissemination of spiritual influences," and the "permeation of community with Christian ideals and principles" for the new birth.[1]

Presbyterian evangelicals waited with interest to catch the reaction of the Board of Foreign Missions to the book. Since the Board had approved the inquiry, and since two of its members were also members of the body that had appointed the Appraisal Commission to act, these evangelicals were anxious to learn of the attitude of the Board and its evaluation of the Commission's assessment of missions. Stonehouse, in his biography of Machen, reports that the Board "failed to utter any ringing disapproval of its central position and contented itself with a vague statement concerning its loyalty to the evangelical basis of the missionary enterprise."[2] In view of the fact that Dr. Lindsey S. B. Hadley, the Board's candidate secretary, was a signer of the *Auburn Affirmation,* it would have been incongruous for that organization to condemn what for years it had been condoning in doctrinal defection.

The second element in the cloud formation was even more explosive.

The talented novelist, Pearl Buck, and her husband, Dr. J. Lossing Buck, were Presbyterian missionary teachers to China. Upon the publication of *Rethinking Missions,* Mrs. Buck applauded its contents with zest: "[It is] The only book I have ever

---

[1]Ned B. Stonehouse, *J. Gresham Machen* (Grand Rapids, Mich.: Eerdmans, n.d.).

[2]Ned B. Stonehouse, *J. Gresham Machen* p. 476.

read which seems to be true in every observation
and right in every conclusion."

In the January, 1933, issue of *Harper's Magazine*,
she made known her views of Jesus in no uncertain
terms:

Even though it is proved in some future time
that there never lived an actual Christ and what
we think of as Christ should be found as the
essence of men's dreams of simplest and beautiful goodness, would I be willing to have that
personification of dreams pass out of men's
minds?. . . Others live it also, many who have
never heard the name of Christ; but to know
the meaning of Christ's life, to know how he
lived and died, is an inestimable support and
help.

In the *Cosmopolitan* for May, 1933, she wrote:

If there existed mind or minds, dreams, hopes,
imaginations, sensitive enough to the human
soul and all its needs, perceptive enough to
receive such heavenly imprint on the spirit as
to be able to conceive a personality like Christ's
and portray him for us with matchless simplic-
ity as he is portrayed, then Christ lives and
lives, whether He was once one body and soul,
or whether He is the essence of men's highest
dreams.

Machen, in a whimsical mood, told his friends of

the futility of trying to get any satisfaction from his correspondence with the Board of Foreign Missions. He said, "I write the Board asking what it proposes to do about Pearl Buck. The Board writes back and says, 'Dr. Speer [the senior secretary] is a very fine man.' I answer, 'I realize Dr. Speer is a very fine man but what I would like to know is what you plan to do about Pearl Buck's public pronouncements.' The Board writes me again and says. 'Machen, why are you so bitter?' "

It was probably purposeful exaggeration. Machen, for some time, wondered how the Board would react to Mrs. Buck's statements. The most he could draw from it was a hazy assurance that members were holding dialogues with her—she was home on furlough that year—and that they hoped to assist her in her theological problems.

Meanwhile, because Mrs. Buck was such a prominent public figure, the press gave considerable publicity to the controversy. Dr. Speer finally admitted that Pearl Buck was under scrutiny. Another secretary, Dr. Cleland McAfee, played the matter down: "We do not take this case so seriously as do some people."

By now the cloud was dropping rain.

What followed is a long and dramatic and sad story. Machen, in clear but respectful rhetoric, petitioned the General Assembly to be careful to elect to the Board of Foreign Missions only Bible-believing persons, to instruct the Board to safeguard the purity of the gospel by carefully screening candidates for missionary service and passing only those who believed in the doctrinal standards of the church, and to warn the Board of the danger of engaging in entangling alliances with union enterprises.

To support his overture, Machen prepared a booklet he entitled, *Modernism and the Board of Foreign Missions.* With characteristic objectivity he produced manuscript evidence to prove that the Board was doctrinally vulnerable and had for some time tolerated and indeed had actually participated in propagating another message than the redeeming gospel of Jesus Christ. The Assembly—the year was 1933—adopted a king-can-do-no-wrong attitude toward the overture and made haste to go on record as giving the Board its "wholehearted, unequivocal, enthusiastic and affectionate recommendation."

The action of the Assembly in white-washing the issue closed the door for any kind of reform, since that body is the highest court in a Presbyterian Church. The conservatives were convinced that there was but one course open to them: to establish a mission board committed to sending out Bible-believing missionaries to preach the gospel of Christ free from compromising links. Machen was elected president and Charles Woodbridge executive secretary. The organization was called The Independent Board for Presbyterian Foreign Missions. The next year, candidates were interviewed, carefully interrogated as to their beliefs, approved, and sent overseas.

The issue that brought Westminster Seminary to birth was in principle the identical issue that made necessary the creation of the Independent Board: a clear-cut, militant testimony to the historic Christian faith. At this point, some of the men who had stood shoulder-to-shoulder with Machen on the Westminster issue demurred. Dr. Macartney and others resigned from the Westminster Board of Trustees. Dr. Allis gave up his post on the faculty. Westminster graduates applying for licensure and ordination in the Presbyterian Church were becoming suspect.

The 1934 the General Assembly declared the Independent Board to be unconstitutional, its members guilty of violating their ordination vows, and therefore subject to discipline. It also ruled that churches were not free to contribute funds to independent projects. The temper of the Assembly was shown when it moved to pass this astonishing pronouncement:

> A church member or an individual church that will not give to promote the officially authorized missionary program of the Presbyterian Church is in exactly the same position with reference to the Constitution of the Church as a church member or an individual church that refuses to take part in the celebration of the Lord's Supper or any other of the prescribed ordinances of the denomination as set forth in Chapter VII of the Form of Government.

To Machen and others, the thrust of the statement was comparable to an edict out of the Vatican. Substantially, it placed the word of man on a parity with, if indeed not above, the Word of God.

Now the cloud had become a thunderhead.

Machen and most of the other members of the Independent Board steadfastly refused to obey the mandate, taking their stand on Scripture and their constitutional rights over against a man-decreed regulation. For this they were disciplined, pronounced guilty, and ejected from the church.

The ironical and tragic feature was that although the issue was doctrinal, under no circumstances was doctrine permitted to be introduced. It was, declared the church authorities, purely a matter of administration.

Cornelius Van Til upon graduation from Calvin College,
1922.

Cornelius and Rena Klooster Van Til, married September 15, 1925.

Van Til taught for one term at Calvin Seminary in 1952.
Dr. Wyngaarden (left), welcomed him at the opening
chapel service.

The Westminster Theological Seminary faculty soon after moving to the present campus. From left to right: Dr. John H. Skilton, New Testament; Prof. Paul Woolley, Church History; Dr. Cornelius Van Til, Apologetics;

Prof. R. B. Kuiper, Practical Theology; Dr. Ned B. Stonehouse, New Testament; Prof. John Murray, Systematic Theology; Dr. Edward J. Young, Old Testament.

Dr. Cornelius Van Til (left), and his successor in apologetics at Westminster, Dr. Robert D. Knudsen.

Van Til with two of his long-time associates: Dr. Hendrik Hart (left), professor of the Association for Advanced Christian Studies (Toronto) and Mr. Harry Schat, a Dutch-American businessman.

Always ready for a good laugh, Van Til here poses in an
Egyptian tarbush brought along by a student.

Van Til, now retired, maintains his study in the library at Westminster Theological Seminary. A photo of his revered teacher, Geerhardus Vos, hangs on the wall.

CHAPTER 14
Orthodox Presbyterianism

Van Til and R. B. Kuiper were not directly involved in the developments in the Presbyterian Church, U.S.A., since they had retained their membership in the Christian Reformed Church. They were, however, vitally concerned. Their strong sympathies lay with the cause of the Independent Board for Presbyterian Foreign Missions.

Van Til's interest was more than academic. He had made it a practice to go out of his way to befriend foreign students, many of them lonely and uneasy in their strange new environment. He also gave hundreds of copies of his writings to them, to missionaries and pastors of multiple denominations on almost every continent.

When the Presbyterian hierarchy unfrocked Machen and others and outlawed the Independent Board, both Kuiper and Van Til were grieved and angry. Their reaction to the proceedings was expressed by Dr. Clarence Edward Macartney:

The action of General Assembly was unjust and unconstitutional in that it amounted to a sentence upon ministers and laymen within the church without a hearing and without a trial, and violates the constitutional liberties of churches, sessions, and individuals in the matter of the work of Christ's Kingdom. . . . Are godly men to be harried, disciplined, censured, persecuted, because they have banded together as Presbyterians to do a good work and give the Gospel to the heathen? God forbid! It is unthinkable!

Those who were driven from the Presbyterian Church, U.S.A., had no alternative but to found a Presbyterian church that would uphold the authority of the Scriptures and proclaim the great redemptive truths contained therein. Others who realized the implications of what had happened turned in their resignations with heavy hearts and threw in their lot with those who had been ejected from the largest Presbyterian body in the world.

On June 11, 1936, one hundred and thirty ministers and ruling elders joyfully assembled in the friendly Reformed Episcopal Church of the Atonement of Germantown, Pennsylvania, signed an act of association, constituted themselves as the Presbyterian Church of America, and elected Machen as first moderator. It was a step of immense significance. For some, it meant relinquishing valuable church property; for others, giving up pension privileges; for still others, the severing of ties with churches of their fathers, friends, and relatives. But to all, it was simply a matter of priority, an echo of the apostolic response: "We ought to obey God rather than men" (Acts 5:29).

What followed was proof of the principle that when men violate one scriptural rule they do not hesitate to set aside another. The leaders of the Presbyterian Church, U.S.A., next deliberately disregarded Paul's injunction to the Corinthian Christians not to go to law before the unrighteous (see 1 Cor. 6:1). They sent representatives before a civil court to petition the court to order the new denomination to drop the name, Presbyterian Church of America. The argument was based on the premise that the name was too closely identified with the name of the denomination it had separated from, and was therefore confusing in the minds of the public. Strange reasoning. It overlooked the fact that denominations such as the Presbyterian Church, U.S. (Southern Church), the Presbyterian Church of North America, and others had coexisted with the Presbyterian Church, U.S.A., for years with no apparent confusion in the minds of people. This the court ignored and ruled in favor of the appeal. Subsequently, the name Orthodox Presbyterian Church was substituted for the name Presbyterian Church of America.

The disrupting turn of events posed another thorny problem for Cornelius Van Til. He had been nourished on the Bible as his primary authority for faith and life, and on the *Heidelberg Catechism* as the secondary standard. Hence a strong emotional attachment for that excellent creed lodged in him. True, he accepted with no mental reservations the statements in the *Westminster Confession of Faith*, the secondary standard of the Orthodox Presbyterian Church.

The burning question in his mind was, where could he be more useful to the broader interests of Christ's kingdom, in the Christian Reformed Church or the Orthodox Presbyterian Church? His own denomination had come of age and was gifted with scholars and clergymen of unusual ability. The new denomination was in its swaddling clothes. One of the disappointing features in connection with the break with the Presbyterian Church, U.S.A., was the paucity of older, more mature ministers who were willing to leave their positions, their pulpits, and their pensions and join forces with a fresh movement. More than that, colossal problems faced the Orthodox Presbyterians.

There was another factor related to Van Til's decision. Westminster Seminary, although not officially under the control of the Orthodox Presbyterian Church, would assuredly be an essential block in its foundation. Van Til was committed permanently to a faculty post second to none in importance. What then should he do with the balance of his life? What was God's will for him?

One is inclined to conclude that by now, having many times in his career found himself at the crossroads, he should have built up an immunity against inner tensions. Not so. It was with sorrow and some misgiving that again he "took the road less traveled by." He transferred his ministerial membership from the Christian Reformed Church to the Orthodox Presbyterian Church. R. B. Kuiper followed his example, and for some of the same reasons.

Meanwhile, Machen, sensing the need of a journal to keep church issues and developments before the Christian public, started and virtually underwrote a monthly magazine, the *Presbyterian Guardian*.

Abraham Kuyper is responsible for the pungent dictum, "Where there is more light there are more shadows." The truth of the metaphor was borne out by the abundance of light that must have flooded the Orthodox Presbyterian Church. But not long after it had taken off, shadows began to gather.

Machen, who had been elected president of the Independent Board, was dislodged from that position due largely to the influence of Rev. Carl McIntire, also a member of the Board. There was no justification for the act. McIntire wrote one of the Independent Board missionaries that Machen was getting too much power. Probably more was behind it than that.

One of the questions that came before the new church was what precise form of secondary standard was to be adopted. The majority, including Machen, Kuiper, Van Til, and Murray advocated a return to the *Westminster Confession of Faith* as it had been structured prior to 1903, when the Presbyterian General Assembly had changed a few of the articles. This action had had the effect of watering down distinctly biblical and Calvinistic doctrines. McIntire and Dr. J. Oliver Buswell, president of Wheaton College, together with a minority of delegates, opposed the change. They wished to retain the form of the Confession as it existed at the time of the break. The Assembly at its November session in 1936, voted for the return to the original form.

Soon after that, McIntire and Buswell raised two extraneous issues.

Fearful lest the doctrine of Christian liberty might be abused, lest some of the brethren might turn liberty into license, the two men advocated incorporating a so-called "total abstinence" clause in the constitution. They forgot that "God alone is Lord of the conscience, and hath left it free from the doctrines and commandments of men, which are, in anything, contrary to His Word: or besides it, in matters of faith, or worship" (*Westminster Confession of Faith*, Chapter 20, Section 1). The attempt to add to the confessional standards failed.

A second issue was equally unnecessary. John Murray had written a series of articles in the *Guardian*, exposing what he saw as the "errors in modern dispensationalism." They were by no means an attack on the doctrine of premillenialism. McIntire, who had started another journal, the *Christian Beacon*, promptly accused Murray of being unfair to his premillenial position. R. B. Kuiper requested space in the *Beacon* to reply to the charge and set the record straight. McIntire refused the request and instead came out with a slashing assault on Westminster Seminary.

The outcome of this sad conflict was that McIntire, Buswell, and a number of ministers and elders left the Orthodox Presbyterian Church and launched another denomination, the Bible Presbyterian Church.

The darkest shadow was yet to fall over the Orthodox Presbyterian Church, Westminster Seminary, and the total Christian community.

Machen was by now living the life of a whirling dervish. How he managed to teach, preach, write, engage in extensive communication, confer with his colleagues, and prepare and deliver a marvelous series of radio sermons on the distinctive doctrines of the Reformed faith made him, like King David, "a wonder to many."

During the 1936 Christmas holidays, he had agreed to visit some of the struggling new churches in the Dakotas. At the time he was afflicted with a severe cold. Members of his family urged him to cancel the engagements and rest. A thoroughly conscientious man, he felt he must keep his word.

While in the act of preaching in the Orthodox Presbyterian Church at Leith, South Dakota, he was stricken with pleurisy. The pastor of the church, the Reverend Samuel Allen, drove him in bitter cold weather to the Bismarck Hospital, seventy-five miles from Leith, where he was to speak once more. By then he was in physical agony. Against the physicians' advice he insisted on going through with his commitment.

He finally submitted to hospitalization. Pneumonia set in.

It was clear to him and to everyone near him that death was imminent. One of the last things he did was to dictate a telegram to John Murray with this final word: "I'm so thankful for active obedience of Christ. No hope without it."

At 7:30 on the evening of January 1, 1937, Machen

entered not only the new year but also his heavenly rest. So passed from the earthly scene one "of whom the world was not worthy."

CHAPTER 15

Westminster Without Machen

Tribute to Machen's worth as a scholar had poured in from unexpected quarters during his lifetime. Walter Lippmann, in his *Preface to Morals*, saluted *Christianity and Liberalism*, with verve. Said he:

It is an admirable book. For its acumen, for its wit, this cool and stringent defense of orthodox Protestantism is, I think, the best popular argument produced by either side in the controversy. We shall do well to listen to Dr. Machen. The Liberals have yet to answer him.

In his Machen biography, Ned Stonehouse quoted Albert C. Diffenbach, an astute Unitarian writer for the *Boston Evening Transcript,* as saying:

Here is a man of distinction in scholarship and of unequal devoutness who for twenty years and more has declared that those who control the power of his communion have repudiated the authentic and official Presbyterian faith in favor of a modernistic emasculation of the pure

Gospel of the Bible and the Reformation. It is a dramatic situation, extraordinary for its utter reversal of the usual situation in a judicial doctrinal conflict. It amounts virtually to this: one man declaring that, in administrative effect, his whole church has become heretical.

Perhaps the most surprising and unexpected eulogy offered after Machen's passing was from Pearl Buck, who wrote in the January 20, 1937, issue of *The New Republic:*

I admired Dr. Machen very much while I disagreed with him at every point. And we had much the same fate. I was kicked out of the back door of the Church and he was kicked out the front door. . . . The man was admirable. He never gave in one inch to anyone.

It has been said that the Lord's workmen are taken away but His work goes on. To Joshua, God said, "Moses my servant is dead; now therefore arise, go over this Jordan. . ." (Josh. 1:2).

After Machen's death—he was fifty-six at his passing—it was not certain upon whose shoulders the mantle of his leadership would fall. The stricken church was too filled with grief to think about a successor. No one person was ambitious for the honor.

Unfortunately, of the five younger men in whom Machen had placed unbounded confidence, three fell away from the church he had loved from its beginning. McAllister Griffiths went over to Carl McIntire; Edwin Rian returned to the Presbyterian church he had left; Charles Woodbridge took a pastorate in an independent church in the South. Only Paul Woolley and Murray Thompson remained in the Orthodox Presbyterian Church.

It is entirely possible that some looked to Cornelius Van Til as Machen's logical successor. The learned apologist did not think so. He had but recently become a Presbyterian. He shied away from administrative tasks. He was aware of his limitations as a church leader. He overemphasized his restrictions in relation to the matter of expressing himself in the complex English language. He felt that he was constitutionally not up to the role of leadership. Therefore he was perfectly content to apply his God-endowed talents and labor in the sphere in which he felt at home: apologetics.

It was not that he was disinterested in the ongoing program of his denomination. He frequently preached in Orthodox Presbyterian churches as well as to Christian Reformed congregations. He was eager to help start new churches on the home mission front. Quietly, without sounding of trumpets, he capitalized on every opportunity to assist his fellow ministers in their struggles.

To the credit of Edwin Rian, before he left the Orthodox Presbyterian Church, he picked up information about an estate in the lovely Chestnut Hill section of Philadelphia. It had belonged to a wealthy sugar executive named Harrison. Rian persuaded the Board of Trustees that the seminary had to put forth a real effort to assure its friends and its foes that the school would not die because Machen had died.

The idea caught on. Enough money was contributed for a down payment, and in the summer of 1937, Westminster Seminary left Pine Street and located on the Harrison estate in Chestnut Hill.

It proved a wise and salutary move. The new campus was lush and spacious. The former carriage house was converted into a library. There the precious volumes that had come from the libraries of the old Princeton professors were filed. John Murray was able to obtain the valuable library of Principal McLeod of the Scottish Free Church, books that contained numerous writings of the English and Scottish Puritans. The library of liberal Auburn Theological Seminary, the very institution where the *Auburn Affirmation* had originated, was put up for sale. Paul Woolley's perceptive eye caught an advertisement in *The New York Times* notifying the public that a rare collection of the Greek and Latin church fathers, published in Paris by Migne a century before, was available. These invaluable books were secured for the seminary library. The Westminster men rejoiced as those who had found great spoil. The riches of Auburn had been captured by the successor to old Princeton.

Westminster Seminary was again to be tested in the furnace of refinement.

Across the Atlantic Ocean, sinister movements were stirring. Nietzsche's *Zarathustra*, Superman, was looking more and more like a beast out of the pit. Barbarism was becoming the order of the day as the Nazis and the Communists tested their relative strength in a fierce engagement in Spain. Adolf Hitler began closing in on one European country after another. An international rape was on. England was drawn into the conflict. It was obvious that sooner or later America would be. Already in 1938–39, the Army and Navy were stepping up recruitment well above peacetime levels. A number of recent seminary graduates entered the chaplaincy.

Naturally, the enrollment at Westminster suffered. At a particularly low point in the history of the school, only thirty students registered. One year, there were two in the graduating class.

The oldest Reformed institution on the Continent, the University of Debrecan in Hungary, informed Cornelius Van Til in the fall of 1938 that it wished to present him with an honorary professorship. The situation in greater Europe was growing more tense daily. Quelling his apprehension, he sailed for Europe, complete with a Latin dissertation he had prepared for the auspicious occasion. He stopped over in Amsterdam and visited various members of the faculty at the Free University.

He had planned to go on to Budapest by train. The plan was interrupted when Hitler's *Wehrmacht* blitzed across Europe, invaded Austria, and captured Czechoslovakia. Van Til was never able to deliver his Latin speech.

It was of course a bitter disappointment. But the Dutch humor was not to be inhibited, serious as the matter was. "Just think," he told friends, "my otherwise immortal oration is forever lost to posterity."

He crossed the English Channel and waited for a ship to bring him to America. Already the German submarines were stalking trans-Atlantic shipping. He feared that war might break out and block his return.

It was not to be. He was happy when he was able to board a liner and return to Rena, Earl, and his duties at the seminary.

CHAPTER 16

Clark, Buswell, and Van Til

Against his emotional grain, Dr. Van Til was about to become embroiled in disputations with his Christian brethren.

His most serious difference was, as he expresses it, with "my good friend Gordon Clark [who] believes in the inerrancy of the Bible."[1]

Dr. Clark had taught philosophy at Wheaton College and Butler University. He was known as a brilliant pedagogue, a resourceful debator, and a theologian of note, even though he had never attended a theological seminary. Upon receiving a call to a congregation in the Orthodox Presbyterian Church, he sought licensure and ordination in his presbytery and passed the required examinations. Thereupon, a complaint was filed in the Presbytery of Philadelphia, signed by twelve ministers and one ruling elder. The complaint stated that:

Clark's views of the incomprehensibility of God, the relation of the intellect to the will and emotions, the relation of divine sovereignty to

---

[1]David Kucharsky, "At the Beginning, God: An Interview With Cornelius Van Til," *Christianity Today* (Dec. 30, 1977) p. 20.

human responsibility, and the offer of the gospel to man were neither in harmony with the Scriptures nor with the *Westminster Confession of Faith*. His errors were said to be the result of a rationalistic method.

Van Til's case against Dr. Clark's formulations was based on Van Til's consistently held teaching that the essential relationship of man to God is of Creator to creature, a relationship that is presupposed and not to be placed under the microscope of human logic to prove or disprove its reality. Clark held that man's knowledge was identical with God's knowledge, qualitatively but not quantitatively. For Van Til, inscrutable mysteries are to be found in Scripture and are to be accepted, even though not understood—mysteries such as the Trinity, God's incomprehensibility, and the relation of divine sovereignty to human responsibility. Clark argued that man possessed the ability to solve the mysteries by logical deduction. Van Til maintained that faulty human reasoning, because of the effects of sin on the mind,was incapable on its own of comprehending God or God's truth. Clark believed that the rule of logic was alike for both the regenerate and the unregenerate.

Van Til's thumbnail sketch of Clark's position was printed in *Christianity Today:*

> . . . he builds his philosophical outlook not simply on the Scriptures as such but on the law of contradiction, which has its classic statement in Aristotle and which to my way of

thinking has turned out to be an eternally static turnpike in the sky.[2]

Interviewer David Kucharsky presses the Dutchman with searching questions:

Clark believes, doesn't he, that the law of contradiction is implicit in Scripture? That is, he holds Christianity to be true because it is the most consistent system. He believes in logic and reason as an ally, and he contends that universally and necessarily we cannot affirm and deny the same thing at the same time and in the same way. What is wrong with that? Doesn't it supply him with a common ground and a neutral access to the unbeliever? Doesn't this aid evangelism?[3]

Van Til:

My concern is that the demand for non-contradiction when carried to its logical conclusion reduces God's truth to man's truth. It is unscriptural to think of man as autonomous. The common ground we have with the unbeliever is our knowledge of God, and I refer repeatedly to Romans 1:19. All people unavoidably know God by hating God. After that they need to have true knowledge restored to them in the second Adam. I deny common ground with the natural man, dead in tres-

---

[2]*Ibid.*
[3]*Ibid.*, 22.

passes and sins, who follows the god of this world. When these people, for whom my wife and I pray constantly, are born anew, as Jesus tells Nicodemus they must be to see or enter the kingdom of heaven, then we have common ground and will together call other spiritually dead people to repentance and life. The primary task is always to win people to the triune God of the Scriptures. It is in this interest that it is every Christian's duty to witness. The Christian ought to do this, "speaking the truth in love."[4]

The ultimate outcome of the controversy was that, for better or worse, the complaint carried. Good men on both sides of the issue felt deeply, and at times some were hurt. Several, discouraged with the trend in the church, left for other communions. Inevitably, scars marked the body for years to come.

Whether Cornelius Van Til tangled with J. Oliver Buswell or J. Oliver Buswell tangled with Cornelius Van Til is irrelevant. They did tangle.

Dr. Buswell, one-time president of Wheaton College, had, to his everlasting credit, taken a bold and unpopular stand on early Presbyterian Church issues. In the latter years of his life he taught at Covenant Theological Seminary in St. Louis. He was a vigorous defender of the Christian faith.

Buswell's approach to apologetics approximated Gordon Clark's. Both accorded a great amount of reasoning power to the naked intellect. But Buswell

---
[4]*Ibid.*

was inductive, while Clark was deductive. Buswell was concerned with the facts of history and the testimony they bore to the truth of Christianity. In a number of sizeable studies, he sought, in similar fashion to Thomas Aquinas, to marshal the facts, and these bare facts would then prove both the existence of God and the truth of revelation. But of course one must posit the freedom of choice or how could anyone judge the facts?

In passing, it may be said that the discriminating scholar, Louis Berkhof, reviewing one of Dr. Buswell's books, declared that he was unable to tell the difference between Buswell's Calvinism and Buswell's Arminianism.

Van Til was quick to point out that Buswell's inductive reasoning led him straight up a blind alley, as does every distortion of Scripture. The Bible portrays man as a free moral agent but never as one who has the power of free choice. "Can the Ethiopian change his skin, or the leopard his spots? Then may ye also do good, who are accustomed to do evil" (Jer. 13:23). "A good tree cannot bring forth evil fruit, neither can a corrupt tree bring forth good fruit" (Matt. 7:18). Said Charles Haddon Spurgeon: "Left to myself, my will is free to do one thing: sin."

Van Til's unswerving, unmovable postulate is that the Christian must argue by "presupposition." It is the very first of his ground rules. Like Tertullian, he claims Christians must contest the very principles of their opponents' position. The only "proof" of the Christian position is that unless truth is presupposed there is no possibility of proving anything at all. It is absolutely essential to use the same principle in apologetics that one uses in theology: the self-attesting, self-explaining Christ of the Scriptures.

It is the term "the self-attesting Christ of Scripture" that runs through Van Til's writings and lectures just as visibly as the scarlet thread that runs through the ropes of the Royal British Navy. The Christian attempts to understand God's world in subjection to the plan of "the self-attesting Christ of Scripture." He interprets the facts and his experience in the light of the revelation of "the self-attesting Christ in Scripture." One must preach with understanding that the acceptance of "the Christ of Scripture" alone can open blind eyes. The system of truth confronts a person in "the Christ of Scripture." Faith in "the self-attesting Christ of the Scriptures," is the beginning, not the conclusion of wisdom.

Those who oppose Cornelius Van Til's apologetics, as much as they may disagree with his method or conclusions, must, if they are honest, concede that he has developed a Christ-centered, Christ-honoring system.

One of the most interesting and complex personalities who studied under Van Til was the late Dr. Edward Carnell. In his student days Carnell inclined strongly and warmly toward Van Til's apologetic. After Westminster, he went on to take post-graduate work at Boston University where he became interested in personalism. In his major work on apologetics, he gave evidence of jettisoning his former convictions and setting up the great judge *reason* as the pivotal point of contact between the Christian believer and the unbeliever. Later, he was to find accommodations with aspects of Karl Barth's theology. The practical result was that he began to function as an ecumenical bridge between evangelicals and neoevangelicals across the country. Installed as president of Fuller Seminary, he followed a similar pattern. In so doing, he set the stage for the inclusivism that has characterized Fuller since his premature death. This inclusivism comes to light in Lindsell's book, *The Battle for the Bible*.

In *The Case for Calvinism*, Dr. Van Til has stated his objection to the two mediating forces represented by Edward Carnell, crisis theology and neoevangelicalism. The title of Van Til's book was originally suggested by a shipboard companion years earlier. The gentleman had been a history professor and had agreed with Van Til on the importance and primacy of Calvin's influence on the history of Protestant thought. Van Til summarized his argument in these words:

> When Paul was confronted with the consummation of Greek thought, he challenged its wisdom in the name of Christ, whom he met on the way to Damascus. And this Christ was the one who died and rose again from the dead, outside the gates of Jerusalem. We cannot do less than Paul did. We dare not curry favor with self-authenticating man. We dare not claim that the Christian story is "in accordance with logic" and "in accordance with fact" in terms of the vision of self-

authenticating man. We must rather call him to repentance. We must insist on his unconditional surrender to the self-authenticating Christ. But we must do it in the interest of his finding himself, of his finding meaning in science, in morality, and in religion. We must do that in the interest of his participation in the victory of the all-conquering Christ.

It may seem that Dr. Van Til was going out of his way, as some have charged, to tilt with windmills after the manner of Don Quixote. It is not true. He was merely trying to apply with gentleness but firmness what Machen had declared at the opening exercises of Westminster Seminary: "We believe that the Christian religion should be proclaimed without fear or favor, and in clear opposition to whatever opposes it, whether within or without the church."

CHAPTER 17
A Trip to the Orient

For many years after World War II, Dr. Van Til visited colleges, universities, and theological institutions to present his message. By now his rewritten syllabus on apologetics was being studied extensively. Lectures based upon it were given in Dutch, French, Spanish, Japanese, Chinese, and Korean.

Frequently he had the opportunity to speak to audiences who not only disbelieved the Christian gospel but also despised that offensive term, Calvinism. He would always begin without relying on gimmicks or flamboyant methods. He was, he said simply, a farm boy who as a child had been brought up to believe the truth of the Scriptures of the Old and New Testaments. Men like himself were sinners before a holy and righteous God. This same God had graciously provided salvation through the obedience and sacrificial death of his Son, Jesus Christ, who was raised from the dead, now reigns in heaven, and who will come again to rule and to judge the world in righteousness.

Against the background of this unvarnished testimony he would then move into a more complex discussion. His suave but pointed method of lecturing often caught non-Christian listeners off-guard. He would sweep through the vast vistas of humanistic philosophy in a matter of minutes and diagnose the kernel of meaning at the basis of the most prolix and profound philosophical thinkers: Plato, Aristotle, Descartes, Schopenhauer, Kant, Mill, Hegel, Bradley, Bosanquet, Dooyeweerd, Brightman. He was at home with each and all.

After hearing one of his lectures, a Jewish student, who had sat enthralled for three hours, said that Dr. Van Til had done more to explain Kant and Hegel to him than his secular professor of philosophy had accomplished in a whole year!

One of the delightful intervals in his busy regime was the summer he and a close friend, Dr. Gilbert den Dulk, a physician from Ripon, California, made a trip to the Orient. It was with unrestricted pleasure that he met and conferred with a large number of his former Westminster students, some of whom had suffered excruciating pain for the sake of their Savior during the Second World War.

This is a description of the trip in his own homespun idiom:

Gilbert and I flew from San Francisco to the Hawaiian Islands. There we landed on the main island and made our way to a small hotel where our sleeping room was on the first floor and our baggage lay next to our beds. Of course we had to take a taxi to see pineapple land and guzzle cold pineapple juice utterly without charge. We heard that a tidal wave was coming; a policeman assured us that this must be true because the waves were coming perpendicularly to the beach rather than horizontally. Who dares doubt a man in uniform about such a matter?

Nothing happened.

Gilbert and I returned to the lobby of our hotel because our plane was to take off after the midnight hour. Because I was going out to Asia to preach, there came to me the words of Paul when he was about to enter Macedonia:

"Now thanks be unto God, which always causeth us to triumph in Christ, and maketh manifest the savor of his knowledge by us in every place. For we are unto God a sweet savor of Christ, in them that are saved, and in them that perish: To the one we are the savor of death unto death; and to the other the savor of life unto life" (2 Cor. 2:14–16).

Our first stop was Tokyo; we visited one of the Buddhist Temples there and saw the Imperial Palace. We flew from Tokyo to Taipei, the capitol of Taiwan. On Sunday morning I preached to a large Chinese Christian congregation. It was in this service that I first sang a hymn in Chinese: *sensai, sensai, sensai* (Holy, Holy, Holy!). A former student of mine, the Reverend Egbert Andrews, for many years a missionary in Taiwan, took me to a large university where I spoke two evenings on the Christian philosophy of life, to more than eighty students.

I then moved on under the care of another

missionary and former student, the Reverend
Richard B. Gaffin, Sr. He gave me several rides
on the back of his motorcycle, which was a new
experience for me. At their home, Mrs. Gaffin
rang a little bell and a Chinese lady produced a
magnificent fish; it was the best of eating for
me.

I then embarked on a local plane to travel to
the southern-most city of Taiwan. As we approached the city, the windowshades of our
plane were drawn shut so as to keep the pas-
sengers from seeing the large American military establishment on the ground below.

I was taken out to a celebration dinner by the
faculty of the theological seminary there. From
soup to nuts, the faculty and I discussed the
theology of Karl Barth; they were all for it, and I
was, of course, against it.

Outside, the heat was semi-tropical and my
appearance was that of a well-cooked lobster.
When I landed, Mrs. Andrews who had come
to meet me, suggested that I return to my hotel
and rest. But her conveyance, Mr. Jeep, refused
to budge, alleging a punctured tire as an excuse. But it was all for the good; I got my first
and only ride in a pedicab, going through the
busy streets, past stands piled high with all of
the vegetables a verdant island could produce,
among hundreds of children and huge trucks
honking their way throughout their endless
comings and goings.

Meanwhile, Gilbert had met a Chinese-
Christian couple in Taiwan. He met them

again in Hong Kong. I had one more meeting at which to speak on Saturday morning, and then I, too, was on my way to Hong Kong. Gilbert had already bought one of Hong Kong's famed suits and a golden-haired jacket.

The hurricane indicator was going up and up; we wondered if it would reach us or if the same thing that had happened to the tidal wave in Hawaii would overtake it.

From Tokyo we went to Seoul, the capital of Korea. President Eisenhower had been invited to visit Tokyo, but the outbreak of many hostile demonstrations changed his plans, and he was to come to Seoul. Gilbert and I were ensconced in a hotel with waiters who spoke English. All of the wooden gods, which had never before felt a coat of paint, were now all fresh and fair. The city was sprayed from stem to stern for mosquitoes and a large banner was displayed in the huge city square with the words: WE LIKE IKE!

A medical missionary was taking us out to the country to see an establishment for orphans—the children of American G.I. fathers and Korean mothers. But it took us well over an hour just to escape the multitudes in the central square. Our driver inched along; children climbed on the hood while adults pressed on both sides of the bus. The trip was accomplished at about three miles per hour. From Seoul we took the train to Pusan. On the way we could see Korean women planting the rice plants in the watery paddies. Out in the darkness we could see the distant lights of towns and here and there a single light bulb in a rural hamlet. I was met at the station by the Reverend Bruce Hunt and taken to the Hunt's commodious compound. Both born in Korea, the Hunts knew the language very well. A ring of the bell at the alley gate permitted us to enter the roomy yard. The back fence was broad and high but still had a line of barbwire running along the top.

For breakfast we had goat's milk and all of the breakfast cereals known to the city of Pusan. Next day Mr. Hunt took me to a large Korean church near his home. I was given a large paper bag of the size that the A & P might use. Of course, I took off my shoes; even so I preferred my own aboriginal footwear. Okay, then, I was given a pair of felt overshoes; so on to the pulpit I went with softly padded feet. But later I walked right out of doors, shoes, over-shoes and all. I thought to myself, "No, no, Van, you are supposed to take them off before you go outdoors," so like the obedient little red hen, I did.

The Korean way is to say it with flowers. Before I could say a single syllable from the pulpit, two little girls about three years of age came forward, each carrying a huge mass of flowers and seating themselves one on my right and another on my left knee. When I showed my obvious approval of this display by my newly found lady friends, I was im-mediately in with the audience. Each day I lectured at 10:00 A.M. and again at 7:00 P.M. and each time to a large gathering. There were, of course, no pews and they were always giving orders: "Please stand up! Please come forward. Room for a hundred more! Please be seated on the floor!" At 5:00 A.M. the church bells were tolling the time for morning prayer.

I had also been invited to speak to the students at the Korean Reformed Seminary. I was all set to show them my great erudition: but it struck me, how do you or I explain the philosophy of the ancient Greek, Heracleitus with his dictum, *"panta rei,"* especially when one is not sure he knows what it means himself?

So I spoke of the saving grace of God in Jesus Christ who died for our sins, who rose for our justification and ascended to glory, there to prepare a dwelling place for all those whom the Father had given him. Never have I had such appreciation for my words nor did I ever see such glistening eyes brimming with tears when they saw Jesus crucified and heard Him cry out in His agony: "My God, My God, Why hast thou forsaken me?"

Have you ever seen and heard a sizeable group of believing Christian men, women, and children pray? I did; the audience was moving in the way that wheat moves when the wind blows over it. "The wind bloweth where it listeth, and thou hearest the sound thereof, but canst not tell whence it cometh, and whither it goeth; so is every one that is born of the Spirit" [John 3:8]. Let no one tell me with dolorous voice that I was beside myself. Of course, what I heard that day in that great church of Christ was not a second Pentecost. Christ is life! He rose from the dead; He ascended to the right hand of the Father, making daily intercession for His people. It was of this faith that these my fellow believers in Korea sang so heartily, and I swayed with them as they sang.

Again, they say it with flowers. At the Pusan airport, as we were about to embark on the flight back to Seoul, the same two little girls brought more flowers. But on the plane the flowers disappeared mysteriously.

Since my wife never accompanied me on these trips because of the expense, I asked before I left, "Mom, can I bring you anything from the Orient?" She did not want anything but a vase, but not too expensive a one. But everywhere we went we were presented with vases. There was always one for Gilbert and one for me, mine was always a bit larger, presumably because I was thought to be Jupiter, the chief speaker.

Back we went to Seoul; back to more elaborate meals. I had one more meeting on Monday morning and this time the sole speaker got not a mere vase but a VASE of huge proportions packed in an ornamental box. All of the vases, small and large, had beautifully inlaid dragons on them and all made of brass. Back to Tokyo, on to Alaska, on to Seattle, on to San Francisco and then to Ripon with Gilbert.

Even though I was exhausted from the trip, it was a great blessing to me to have seen the students I had taught over the years— missionaries and natives of the countries. I saw first hand their congregations and their students and the continual spread of the gospel to new generations and to new areas no man could ever have reached by himself in a lifetime.

CHAPTER 18
Van Til and Barth

The trip to the Far East contributed more than anything to opening Cornelius Van Til's eyes to the need of earthy, instructive material that would help pastors and missionaries find their way through a maze of sometimes awesome quandaries in the region of modern philosophy and theology. He was made to realize afresh that the minds of Chinese, Japanese, and Korean young people, exposed as they are to all shades of mysticism and relativism, had to be insulated against man-made systems of thought, and to be encouraged, positively, to pyramid their own faith on the impregnable Rock of truth—intelligently, lovingly, and consistently.

Out of his experiences in the Orient was born his *Defense of the Faith,* which he considers to be his most important book. Actually, it is a rewriting and reediting of some of his former syllabi. While putting together the material, he tried to keep in mind certain problems of the student, pastor, and missionary. His friends believe that many of his keenest and most penetrating thoughts come across in this volume.

Another interesting and quite startling discovery

that came home to him during his contacts in the Far East was the wide influence of Karl Barth. Returning to the States, he wrote articles for the magazine *Torch and Trumpet* (now the *Outlook*) and for the *Westminster Theological Journal*. In these he sought to point up the contrast between Barth's complicated and confusing Christology and the clear biblical statements of the person of Christ set forth in the Chalcedon Creed.

Then in 1962, he published his most complete and exhaustive treatment of Barth's theology in *Christianity and Barthianism*. It represents Van Til's concentrated study of the Swiss scholar for a period of forty years. Many find the 450-page book difficult to understand for Van Til continuously quotes from the German originals of Barth's writings. The summary of this work demonstrates numerous precedents of Van Til's own thoughts:

> The choice must therefore be made between Barth and the Reformers. On Barth's view there is no transition from wrath to grace in history. And on Barth's view grace is inherently a meaningless idea. For his Christ is composed of the interaction between a principle of continuity based on the idea of timeless being and a principle of discontinuity based on the idea of pureicontingency. He has therefore no gospel of grace to present to man. He cannot challenge men by presenting them with the Christ of the Scriptures because his Christ is a mirage. It is the Christ of modern recon-

struction. It is the Christ of the higher humanism.

The late J. Gresham Machen was confronted with the Christ of the higher humanism in his day. In 1924 he published his book, *Christianity and Liberalism.* In it he pointed out that "the great redemptive religion which has always been known as Christianity" was "battling against a totally diverse type of religious belief, which is only the more destructive of the Christian faith because it makes use of traditional Christian terminology." Said Machen, "The chief modern rival of Christianity is liberalism." An examination of the teachings of liberalism in comparison with those of Christianity will show that at every point the two movements are in direct opposition. The two religions, argued Machen, have mutually exclusive views of Jesus the Christ: "The liberal Jesus, despite all the efforts of modern psychological reconstruction to galvanize Him into life, remains a manufactured figure of the stage." The two religions, argued Machen, therefore also have mutually exclusive views of grace. Having diverse views of sin they naturally have opposite views of grace. A cardinal doctrine of modern liberalism is that the world's evil may be overcome by the world's good; no help is thought to be needed from outside the world.

When Machen found himself compelled thus to speak of liberalism as having denied in fact, though having confessed in word, the gospel of the grace of God in Christ, he did not do so from personal animosity. He did so from a deep desire in his heart that liberals might return to an acceptance of the grace of God in Christ as the only way of salvation for man and his world. If then we are forced by the facts of the case to think of Barthianism, for all its speaking of "election in Christ," as being, like liberalism, a religion of man's own devising, we too, like Machen, must do so from a sincere desire for the salvation of men through the Christ of the Scriptures. Speaking as objectively as we can, we must say that, as in Machen's time, liberalism while propagated in the church as though it were the gospel, was in reality a man-made religion, so Barthianism, using the language of Reformation theology, is still only a higher humanism.[1]

This simple explanation of Machen's attitude toward the destructive though accommodating errors of his day was a commentary on Van Til's own fierce antagonism to the highly intellectualized but appealing unbelief that had become so deceptive to many.

Unfortunately, some readers of *Christianity and Barthianism,* including Barth himself, misunderstood the thrust of the Westminster professor's analysis and concluded that the author was en-

---

[1]Van Til, *Christianity and Barthianism* (Nutley, N.J.: Presbyterian & Reformed, 1962), pp. 445–446.

gaged in a personal attack on Karl Barth. Nothing was more remote from the truth.

Soon after *Christianity and Barthianism* was released, William Jones, a warm friend and admirer of Cornelius Van Til, was driving along a street in Princeton when he happened to spot the continental theologian hurrying to keep a probable appointment. Jones braked his car and called out, "Dr. Barth, may I take you somewhere?"

Barth looked up, surprised, and said in broken English, "T'ank you very much, yes."

He got into the car and explained where he wished to go.

Jones said, "Dr. Barth, I'm a friend of Cornelius Van Til. I must say you and he are great scholars, even though you disagree in your convictions."

Karl Barth frowned and said, "Ach, he hates me."

"No sir, he doesn't hate you or anybody else," Jones protested. "I happen to know he often prays for you."

Barth was deeply moved. "I am glad to know that," he said quietly.

CHAPTER 19

South of the Border

In the early years of Westminster Seminary, Dr. Van Til had taught a student named David Brainard Legters. He was graduated in 1935, and subsequently labored for years as a linguistic missionary under the banner of the Presbyterian Church of Mexico. In 1962, Mr. Legters invited his former professor of apologetics to visit the Yucatan Province.

Van Til's pilgrimage to Mexico is best told in his own words:

Mrs. Legters met me and took me north to see the ruins of the Aztec Indian civilization. The ruins indicate that once there had been huge stone structures; yet on the way I saw nothing but open huts and no growth other than hemp. Then on to the Province of Tabasco and the city of Paraiso at the very south of the Gulf of Mexico. Here were luscious avocados—almost, but not quite, within my reach. Every man had a transistor radio and the young men promenaded the city square in one direction while the young ladies promenaded

in the opposite one. A huge Roman Catholic
cathedral dominated the city's center and filled
it with light while the outer circumference was
filled with darkness.

Until 12:00 A.M. fire crackers went off every
hour on the hour. At 5:00 A.M. the master
rooster crowed loudly. [here Van Til will give a
most surprising but most convincing cock
crow]; soon his many men-servants picked up
the song and imitated their lord and master in
an awful din.

The General Assembly of the Mexican Presbyterian Church was holding their annual
meeting. It was to this gathering that I was to
speak. There was no restriction on meals, and
tortillas and red beans constituted the noon-
day meal. I had seen the great red cow car-
casses hanging in the streets as we made our
way to the place. Of course Sunday required a
special treat; accordingly, someone went and
bought two turkeys. In a space behind the back
entrance these two gobblers were reduced to
savory meats along with other flavorful
goodies. They were such that all ruling and
specially *teaching* elders greatly enjoyed them.

At my host's urging, one of the kind cooks
brought me an egg, peeled it and wiped it on
her apron. Being a fastidious Dutchman, I be-
sought my hostess to inform the aforesaid
madam that I was completely capable of
handling the product of a hen and peeling it
myself without any help whatsoever.
Moreover there was a loaf of beautiful white

bread which Mrs. Legters cut into pieces for me.

At tea-time one of the female helpers came with a huge bucket of a cold soft drink. Lest some should miss out on the sweetness that lay at the bottom, she proceeded to stir this delicate mixture with her arm. Everybody drank great draughts except C. Van Til, whose thirst was adequately quenched by the action of the virtuous woman.

Bananas! Bananas! Bananas! I discovered a huge pile lying near the cemetery; I appropriated to myself as many as I wished. I lost only three pounds that week, with the consequence that my figure and even my temper improved remarkably.

I had been invited to give lectures at the Christian Reformed Seminary of Mexico. It was good to hear faithful men, faculty and students alike, go out into the villages and byways to call men to repentance. Even though literacy was not high, many of them left small booklets, each containing the gospel of sovereign grace through Jesus Christ, crucified, risen from the dead and ascended to glory. I also preached each evening and Mrs. Legters relayed my message into Spanish, which she spoke as fluently as English. Of course, I knew Spanish as well as any and I conveyed this to the audience by giving forth in song, *sancta, sancta, sancta* in no uncertain sound.

Cornelius Van Til realized with increasing dis-

may that the theology of Karl Barth was sweeping
not only the Oriental countries but also the Latin
American world. A number of evangelical church
leaders were unaware of the fact that Barth was
responsible for a mass of literature tinted with
post-Kantian philosophy. They simply did not
know how to respond to him and were not sure
whether his ideas were a bane or a blessing. Van
Til's ministry to this cross-section of good and
hungry men was to show them that Barth's theology was to be traced back to its root-origin. Long
before Karl Barth or Emil Brunner or Paul Tillich
were born, there had been the centuries-old conflict between the Christian faith and secular
philosophy—first as it appeared in the pages of the
Bible and later as the Latin church accommodated
its teachings to speculative Greek thought. But it
was fundamentally the synthesis of Kant and Hegel
that Van Til found to be the bedrock foundation of
European scholarship. From Europe, camouflaged
in clever and deceptive language, it filtered into
North and South America and was hailed as neo-
Calvinism—this to the great confusion of masses of
professing Christian people.

Van Til continues and concludes the report of his
journey to the land south of the border:

> I had been invited to speak specifically on
> the significance of the theology of Barth to the
> audience in Mexico City. I spoke for an hour on
> the background to Barth's theology and then
> another hour on the specifics of his own sys-
> tem of theology.

The audience was divided. One Mexican clergyman passed around two sheets of paper in Spanish to every one in attendance. It stated that I was a disturber of the peace, and asked why the Mexican church should import a man to attack the great man of God, Barth. After all, the Princeton faculty believed in him and so did Billy Graham so how could I attack the center of a revival of true theology. But I was not without a defender. I have forgotten his name, but with a stentorian voice one man stood up and declared: "Van Til *contra mundum!*" I did not really fancy myself to be Athanasius reincarnate, but I was sorry to see this flourishing church already inundated by a gospel which was not a gospel. And thus ended another journey to the mission field.

CHAPTER 20

A Controversial Apologist

In 1953, a four-volume work of great importance was published in the English language, *The New Critique of Theoretical Thought*. The author, the late Herman Dooyeweerd, a brilliant Dutch lawyer and a major modern philosopher, taught at the Free University at Amsterdam. The publication of the book opened new horizons and started new trends in the Reformed community. Because he worked with philosophical ideas more than with theological propositions and because some of his principles seemed puzzling to theologians, Dooyeweerd came under heavy fire. His motives became suspect. He was not constitutionally tempered to shrug off criticisms, but he felt that in good conscience he must defend his views. In consequence, tensions, not altogether unhealthy, polarized men of Reformed persuasion.

One factor that led to this polarization was semantic misunderstandings. Dooyeweerd relied on a very precise vocabulary best known to the inner circle at the Free University, while American students of theology were oriented to a vocabulary quite different from the Dooyeweerdian school of thought.

Dr. Dooyeweerd came to America in 1959 for a lecture tour. He spoke at Calvin Seminary, the University of Pennsylvania, Westminster, and other institutions. The major theme of the series was "The Christian Doctrine of Man." His approach was more philosophical than exegetical.

Thirty years prior to his visit, Van Til had met him in Holland. At that time the Westminster teacher had been enthusiastic about the fresh new voice in the Reformed society. Increasingly, however, as he read the lawyer's writings and corresponded with him, he discovered that some of their basic convictions did not coincide. When Dooyeweerd was in Philadelphia they held an interview. It did nothing to bring the two closer together.

A second factor that possibly added to the polarity that separated Dooyeweerd and Van Til was that it is doubtful that either scholar had the time or energy to do justice to the other's positions, with their profundities and complexities. Both men turned out massive amounts of material in their respective fields. Both had commitments to teach, lecture, write, and perform other pressing duties. To make matters worse, they were separated by the long years of the war.

The problem of communication comes out in *Jerusalem and Athens.* Says the jurist: "I am afraid you have misunderstood what I mean by this distinction [i.e., the distinction between a transcendental and a transcendent criticism]. By a transcendent criticism, as opposed to a transcendental critique of theoretic thought, I understand something quite different from what you suppose. The first point can now be considered as resting on a misunderstanding."[1]

Dooyeweerd proceeds to accuse Van Til of holding "a typical rationalistic scholastic tendency in your theological thought." He continues, "It seems to me that it is again a certain rationalistic view of the divine Word-revelation that hinders you from seeing the fundamental difference and the true relation between the central religious and the theoretical-conceptual sphere of knowledge. Your terminology is not always clear to me."[2]

Van Til struggles through thirty-eight pages in an effort to reply to Dooyeweerd.

Summarizing his argument, Van Til protests that his 'system' is not that of empiricism, of rationalism, of criticism, or any other "systems" the lawyer may read about in the ordinary texts on philosophy. "Nor is my 'system' a synthesis between one of your systems with that of the Bible. My 'system' is attained by thinking upon all the aspects of reality in the light of the Christ of Scripture. I try to think God's thoughts after Him. . . . an analogical reinterpretation of the truth that God has revealed about Himself to man through Christ in Scripture."[3]

He concludes, "I hope too that the interchange of ideas between us may help others, after us, to listen more carefully to the words of the self-attesting Christ of Scripture in order that they may better

---

[1]Robert Geehan, ed., *Jerusalem and Athens* (Nutley, N.J.: Presbyterian & Reformed, 1971) p. 74
[2]*Ibid.*
[3]*Ibid.*, p. 126.

bring the word of truth to all men everywhere—all to the praise of our triune God. Soon we shall meet at Jesus' feet.''

A second voice more disturbing to Van Til than the voice of Herman Dooyeweerd came from a younger man in the department of theology at the Free University, Harry M. Kuitert. Kuitert did not overthrow all the tenets of the Reformers, but he did tone down some of them. He sought to be "relevant" to the social realities and the young people of his generation. He was particularly vocal in his support of the European student movement in its opposition to the presence of American troops in Viet Nam. He also involved himself vigorously in current political and social problems. But what concerned Van Til more than anything was Kuitert's liberal view of Scripture generally and of the historical portions of Genesis particularly.

Kuitert paid a visit to America. Harry Schat, a businessman and a member of the Christian Reformed Church, thought it would be helpful to bring Kuitert and Van Til together. He arranged meetings between the two scholars. It was a futile experiment that ended in frustration. Although both were cordial, courteous, and gentlemenly, neither would budge from his stance. Kuitert could not understand Van Til's attachment to what Kuitert thought was stifling traditionalism, and Van Til was at a loss to understand Kuitert's liberalized accommodation to modern trends in theology. They parted with goodwill, but each was more firmly convinced than ever that he was right in his beliefs.

By now it will be seen that Van Til is a controversial figure. Undoubtedly, some will assume that in his own mind he has regarded himself as a twentieth-century Elijah: ". . . I, even I only, am left . . ." (1 Kings 19:10).

This is an inevitable misunderstanding. Controversialists have always been marked men. They said of Christ, who was constantly stirring the waters of disputation, ". . . He is beside himself." (Mark 3:21.) Paul suffered periods of loneliness: "At my first answer [defense] no man stood with me . . ." (2 Tim. 4:16). In Geneva, residents named their dogs after John Calvin. Spurgeon was regularly vilified. Machen, in the hour of his most bitter persecutions, wrote his brother: "I am overwhelmed almost beyond endurance."

Kees Van Til shares the companionship of a limited but valiant company.

CHAPTER 21

"What Do You Do With
a Naked Atheist?"

The image of Dr. Cornelius Van Til would not really be complete unless one saw or visualized him in action in the classroom.

In his initial year at Princeton Seminary he shyly went before the class in junior apologetics, unsure of himself, a public lecturer who gave the impression he wished he had gone over his material more thoroughly. He fielded questions from the students hesitantly, almost apologetically.

A decade later at Westminster he came across as self-confident, knowledgeable, exciting, witty, able to fire back answers at enquiring students boldly and pointedly. An electric current seemed to flow from the podium where he stood, stalked, gestured, pirouetted, and expounded his theories with animation.

The Westminster seminarian's introductory view of the eminent doctor invariably produced something of a surprise. The slender Van Til, trained and disciplined on the farm, breezed into the classroom like the original Flying Dutchman. Neatly arrayed in a business suit with a white shirt and solid-colored or striped tie, his hair was rumpled from the treatment of the wind or from the exertion of getting there on time. He deposited a pile of books and manuscripts on the table and paused to begin the period with a brief prayer. Then towering over rows of international youth, he plunged into his subject for the day.

This routine would vary from time to time. Instead of starting the class on a lecture note, sometimes he would point a finger at a student and ask, "Does television bring you nearer to God?" Or, "Do you think Socrates deserved the death penalty?" On one occasion he asked a yearling, "What would you do with a naked atheist?"

The quick reply cracked up the professor and brought howls of delighted laughter from the students: "I'd put some clothes on him."

He was the most informal of pedagogues. He had no set form or pattern on the platform. He would whisper, shout, wheedle, admonish, throw erasers and wads of paper around the podium, and crack jokes. Once he said, "I am tempted to sing a song I learned from my grandfather." A voice from the rear called out, "Yield not to temptation." He fired an eraser at the maverick.

On a memorable morning a young man from Switzerland raised his hand and propounded a question. Van Til, toying with a piece of pointed chalk, figured it was a silly question. Impulsively, he hurled the chalk at the inquirer, striking him on the forehead. Unknown to the lecturer it drew blood. The next morning the victim showed up in a crash helmet.

In the December, 1977, issue of *Christianity To-*

day, Grady Spires, associate professor at Gordon College, has a fitting description of C. Van Til in typical form:

> Van Til, the pedagogical performer, proved as vigorous in lecture and discussion as the polemics of his writing would suggest. Every student of Van Til can instantly recall the characteristic Van Tillian blackboard graffiti: the foremost symbol being two circles, a big one for the creator, the other for creation with no ontological bridge between. The entire history of philosophy or Christian thought, including most heresy, would be strewn in names and phrases across the board. He scrawled Latin, Greek, German, and Dutch wherever there was room. By the time he finished lecturing his hands, his clothes, and even his face would be chalk-smudged.

Spires's picture is not overdrawn. Van Til's favorite platform tools were a blackboard and either white or colored chalk. He and chalk were Siamese twins.

The podium blackboard revealed an amazing series of diagrams. Starting simply and innocently with two or three lines, they expanded into a network of concentric circles, squares, parallelograms and ellipsoids. For some time the neophyte who had been exposed to a shallow philosophical background sat quivering like gelatin in an earthquake before this madcap barrage of learning.

David Kucharsky was right when he stated,

"Like most great thinkers he [Van Til] is not easy to understand." One reason is that it requires time and some effort on the part of the listener or reader to take in his unique method of presentation. It is like a grapeshot, flecking out in different directions and covering a large perimeter of thought.

His illustrations, too, call for a certain amount of digestion before they are absorbed by the student. He wishes to show how a Christian apologist should, for argument's sake, put himself in the position of an unbeliever in order to point out to the unbeliever that he must presuppose the truth of Christianity in order to oppose it. He says he saw a little girl on a train sitting on her father's lap slapping him in the face. If the father had not held her on his lap she would not have been able to slap him.

Phenomenalism—the doctrine developed by Hume (and further developed in a different sense by Kant) which says that concepts present in the mind are the *only* objects of knowledge—Van Til compares to the creation of an island of rationality that has been built up by taking dirt from its center and patching it on its sides, as the Chicago lake front was built up with dirt hauled from the land; the phenomenalists have no right to think of a bottom underneath the water into which they throw their dirt.

The intellect of fallen man, says Van Til, is like a sharp and shiny, buzz saw. Unknown to the owner of the saw, his little son has tampered with the saw and changed its set. Result: Every board he saws is cut slantwise and therefore unusable. The effect will always be the same so long as the set of the saw remains unchanged. When the gospel is presented to the natural man it will be cut according to the set of sinful personality—the keener the intellect, apart from regeneration, the more consistently will the truth of Christianity be cut according to a self-made pattern.

Once the student or reader gets hold of Van Til's approach things begin to fall into place. And to young people whose university or college education has been programed along humanistic lines it is a blessed relief to realize there is an intellectual respectability and defensibility founded on a childlike faith in Jesus. After all, the apostle wrote, ". . . not many wise men after the flesh, not many mighty, not many noble, are called (1 Cor. 1:26); he did not say, "not *any* wise, mighty, or noble." Moreover, he counseled the Roman Christians: "I would have you wise unto that which is good, and simple concerning evil" (Rom. 16:19). The intellectual is just as desperately in need of the gospel of grace as the unlearned and uneducated.

Dr. Van Til's examinations were something his students cannot forget.

On a certain examination day he raced breathlessly into the classroom as the bell sounded. He paused to pray and then began to lecture. An intrepid student apologized for interrupting him and said, "Dr. Van Til, today we have our examinations." He whirled around, took a piece of chalk from his pocket, and wrote on the blackboard, *ankennungsfungpunkt*. He said spiritedly, "Well, write on that," and vanished like the genie in *Arabian Nights*. The "that" was the German philosophical term for "point of contact problem."

One of the very helpful and profitable features of his teaching was the question and answer interlude. At times the discussion would take on a rough-and-tumble dimension, but as a rule it was good fun and conducted in an atmosphere of good will. On rare occasions an intellectual superstar would challenge Van Til's position. The two would wrestle over the point, while lesser lights would sit by confused with open mouths. Yet when the battle of words waxed hottest, Van Til had a way of keeping his temper in check. He managed to end the conflict smiling.

Like Machen, Van Til always found time to confer with seminarians oppressed with doubts or burdened with other problems. Frequently, students, alumni, and people acquainted with his writings—but who had never met him—would ask for an interview. His home was always open.

It is an interesting fact that those who had not met him before would come away shaking their heads. They would say, in so many words, "We can't believe it. From his books we had the idea he was a Samson, smiting hip and thigh those who disagreed with him. Instead we found him as meek as Mary's little lamb, as well as gracious, humble, and kind."

CHAPTER 22

Van Til and His Critics

The noted fifteenth-century Italian sculptor Donatello confessed that he did his best work at Florence, where he was abused and criticized, and not at Pisa, where he was praised and where he became lazy and self-satisfied. Thus, criticism may function as a physician of value if one will accept the prescribed therapy.

It has already been pointed out that Van Til was faulted by friend and foe either for being unfair to those who disagreed with his apologetic, or for his unbending posture. However, Van Til accepted criticism with a gracious and gentle spirit.

Early in his teaching career, a caustic satirist torpedoed him with the burst: "Cornelius Van Til's philosophical teachings are miasmatic exhalations of a false intellectualism." Van Til shrugged it off with a grin and continued to go about his work.

Another critic of Van Til is Dr. John Warwick Montgomery, a Lutheran scholar, a prolific reader and writer, and a contributor to the *Festchrift*, *Jerusalem and Athens*. In his article he attempts to pull the proverbial rug from under Van Til's feet. He does this cleverly with the use of three fables.

The fables are supposed to reveal how thoroughly Van Til's apologetic, with its presuppositional foundation, fails to accomplish its purpose.

Montgomery reasons that we must start, continue, and end our apologetic with the brute facts. Non-Christian positions must be smoked out and the Christian position established factually. He writes:

> With the apostle Paul we must become all things to all men—operate on the non-Christian's territory even as our Lord was willing to incarnate himself in our alien world. . . . The evidence of Christianity's truth has never been closeted in a presuppositional corner; it has always been in public domain, capable of examination by all. As such, it must be brought to bear on the unbeliever, so that he will indeed stand naked, without excuse, under the sheer pressure of incarnational fact. [1]

The procedure, Montgomery insists, must be none other than the inductive method, for Christian as well as for non-Christian.

Montgomery then goes on to drop this bomb: "There is no doubt that apologetes like Van Til treat the non-Christian very much as if he were Christian." He follows this detonation with a second bomb: "Strange to say, this is also Barth's method —though for different reasons."

---

[1] Robert Geehan, ed., *Jerusalem and Athens* (Nutley, N.J.: Presbyterian and Reformed, 1971), p. 390.

How does Van Til receive Dr. Montgomery's criticism?

First, he commends his critic for the highly imaginative and delightful style of the article.

Second, he takes the approach Dr. Montgomery has adopted, traces it back in its historical sweep to Socrates, to Kant, to Robert Collingwood, to Barth, and finally to Bultmann, and shows how in every instance the principle of relying on *inwardness* has failed to bring men to the truth as it is in Jesus. Collingwood clearly defines the terminus of this method when he says, "If an historian took the statements of Jesus about himself at face value, he would disqualify himself as an historian."[2]

Van Til then turns to John Warwick Montgomery and asks, "Do you know any school of modern philosophy that allows for the possibility of the truth of the Christian story as Luther and Calvin believed in it? I know not one."[3]

Third, Van Til responds to parable with parable. He illustrates his argument by dramatizing an imaginary dialogue between Dr. Martin Luther and Dr. Martin Marty, a modern liberal theologian, with Dr. Montgomery sitting in as an auditor.

The dialogue is too lengthy to quote. Van Til tries to draw a definitive line between the process employed by the liberal school and his own. He concludes the piece by having Martin Luther say to Martin Marty:

Well, then, as to our common friend

[2]*Ibid.*, p. 391.
[3]*Ibid.*, p. 392ff.

Montgomery? I not only think, but I am certain
he is on my side. I heard him singing *Ein Feste
Burgh* too. However, he seems to think that he
can at the same time also be on your side. He
does not seem to realize that his inductive
method, as he uses it in common with the
non-Christian analytic-positivists, implies, as
it is implied by, a metaphysics of pure chance.
I hope he won't continue to try straddling the
fence. Don't you think I may, as an old man,
call upon him to forsake a position in which
men may be saved or damned 'without God's
knowing anything at all about it'? As it is he
looks like one of the Liliputian rope-dancers,
divided into two parts, each part rushing into
the other seeking to destroy it.[4]

Dr. G. C. Berkouwer, one of the shining
luminaries in the galaxy of Dutch theologians,
known universally for his writings, has also
criticized Van Til. In his contribution in the
Festschrift, Berkouwer affirms his complete confidence in "the absolute authority of Scripture."
"Holy Scripture," he says, "is the infallible Word of
God, reliable in all respects, and the one and only
rule for our faith. In this there is not a single difference between Van Til and me."

What then, in Dr. Berkouwer's eyes, is the weakness in Dr. Van Til's system? Principally, it lies in
his inconsistency.

In his book on *The Sovereignty of Grace*, Van Til
admits that exegesis of Holy Scripture must play a

---
[4]*Ibid.*

decisive role in all our investigations. Well and good. The fact that Van Til is a philosopher and dogmatician and professedly not an exegete, Berkouwer says, does not diminish his responsibility to occupy himself with the *interpretation* of Scripture. Then, Berkouwer charges, if exegesis is to play such a decisive and important role in determining what is true and what is not, it seems passing strange that there has been on Van Til's part "a total lack of biblical reflection and the absence of a *reply* to all the exegetical questions brought forward by Ridderbos, Holwerda, Veenhof, and even myself."

Dr. Berkouwer says that there are other points of disagreement between himself and Van Til, such as their respective assessment of Karl Barth's theology. But he is willing to bypass these disagreements in order to get to the heart of what he believes to be the vulnerable feature of Van Til's apologetic.

Van Til graciously acknowledges his appreciation to Berkouwer for his contribution to the *Festchrift*. He then says:

I agree that my little book on *The Sovereignty of Grace* should have had much more exegesis in it than it has. This is a defect. The lack of detailed scriptural exegesis is a lack in all my writings. I have no excuse for this. . . . With the greatest respect for your work and that of Dooyeweerd, and, I pray, with proper humility, I must say the danger of traditionalism is present with all of us. If I now have the temerity of trying to go 'Beyond' Dooyeweerd and you in the matter of presenting the gospel to modern man, I do so because I think the Christ of the Scripture compels me to do so. I wish I could have given better exegetical justification for this position than I have, but, every bit of exegesis of Scripture already involves a view of the nature of Scripture. We all see through a glass darkly. We must seek to state the truth in love. But I cannot change what is in print. I can, therefore, only apologize for any unduly harsh judgment I have expressed on the work of those who with me seek to make the Christ of the Scriptures known unto men for the solution of their problems.[5]

Cornelius Van Til has profited from his sojourn in Florence, probably more than from his dwelling in Pisa.

---

[5]*Ibid.*, p. 203.

CHAPTER 23

The Renaissance Man

"The good use this world in order that they may enjoy God, but the evil use God in order that they may enjoy this world," said Augustine in his monumental *City of God.*

Dr. Van Til has put a great deal of thought into the subject about which he has written in *Common Grace.* Common grace, he teaches, is to be distinguished from special grace in that all people everywhere, whatever their spiritual state, receive in varying measure God's bountiful provisions. ". . . he maketh his sun to rise on the evil and on the good, and sendeth rain on the just and on the unjust" (Matt. 5:45). "The LORD is good to all, and his tender mercies are over all his works" (Ps. 145:9).

Van Til does not regard this truth in the sense of a mere theological abstraction. Like Paul, he believes that God gives his children all things richly to enjoy. That includes cultural blessings: good music, great art, the beautiful and complex world of nature. "For all things are yours . . . And ye are Christ's, and Christ is God's" (1 Cor. 3:21,23) is superlatively and gloriously true. C. S. Lewis laid out some unbiblical propositions, unfortunately, but he also laid out some good things. One is Lewis' observation that the autocratic mandate of "handle not, taste not, touch not" disapproved of by Paul in Colossians is more Buddhist than Christian. Lewis was right.

One of the first purchases Kees Van Til made when he began to earn wages was to invest in the so-called Five Foot Shelf, a choice selection of the classics. Sometimes he borrows a quotation from Shakespeare, for whom he nurses boundless admiration. He also, in leisure moments, tries to keep abreast of the literature of the nineteenth and twentieth centuries. His students were not surprised when in class he would quote from Kafka, Bernard Shaw, Sherwood Anderson, Sartre, Faulkner, Dostoyevsky's *Grand Inquisitor,* or perhaps a line from Beckett's *Waiting for Godot.* He is particularly interested in modern plays and works of fiction as they relate to the existential movement.

His love of art is passionate. He recalls with unalloyed pleasure his visit to the magnificent Museum Island in Berlin on his return trip to Europe. In Paris he went to the Louvre, where he marveled at the historical paintings from the era of the Revolution and the Napoleonic Wars down to the present century. The view of the Mona Lisa and the rooms dedicated to Delacroix and the modern artists—he took them all in stride.

In Italy, he invaded the galleries at Milan. In Rome, he spent all the time he could in the Vatican Museum with its wealth of Medieval and Renaissance paintings. His most fascinating experience was in the hours he passed in the Sistine Chapel. He says he is still filled with wonder that borders on disbelief when he thinks about the sacred scenes done on the ceiling of the chapel by the incomparable Michaelangelo.

From the Sistine Chapel he wandered through the cavernous St. Peter's Cathedral, stood reflectively in St. Peter's Square, toured the Appian Way, the Catacombs, the ancient Forum, and the Colosseum.

He touched Belgium only long enough to see the Flemish paintings at Bruges and Brussels.

But it was in Amsterdam, the queen city of his native land, that he approached ecstacy. Again and again he would return to the *Rijksmuseum,* one of the great centers of art in the world. He was captivated by the enormous vision, the psychological penetration of Rembrandt Van Rijn in his moving portrayals of scenes from Scripture. He paused at length before the famous Night Watch, studying the shadings and nuances.

There in the Royal Museum also has been collected the works of Franz Hals, and the evocations by Jacob van Ruisdael, of Dutch farm lands, the polder with its cool, gray clouds overhanging and silvery sunlight penetrating the fair landscape. The priceless collections of Holland's golden age, the seventeenth century, are all there: the solid houses and narrow canals of Calvinist *Delft* with its *Oude Kerk* and *Nieuwe Kerk* by Johannes Vermeer, together with countless other masterpieces. Van Til mentally photographed, developed, and stored these in his mind.

In the United States, no less than in Europe, whether the city is Philadelphia, New York, Chicago, Los Angeles, or Walla Walla, the man always likes to take a break from his pressing schedule and wander through a museum.

Another one of Van Til's cultural enjoyments is music. He favors the baroque with its precise rhythm and contrapuntal harmonies. Mrs. Van Til inclined toward Beethoven; her husband likes Bach, especially the chorals and oratories. The Van Til radio is attuned exclusively to classical music. Visitors to the Van Til home will see a small organ in the living room, and will be invited to sit down and play.

Kees' friends have tried unsuccessfully to interest him in sports. Perhaps in a moment of psychological weakness he may tell of the time a golf addict browbeat him into going to the links to see what he could do with clubs and tantalizing little white ball. He says he stood at the first tee, swung at the ball, and sent it soaring straight down the fairway just like a professional. A chorus of admiring "oh's" and "ah's" went up. He birdied the first hole. After that the maddening little dimpled ball just lay on the fairway and sneered at him. He gave up the sport and vows that he will never get back on the course.

On the serious side, the church he attends regularly, the Calvary Orthodox Presbyterian Church of Glenside, wanted to honor him on his seventy-fifth birthday. This posed a problem, since he is in truth "the man who has everything," even though he lives simply.

Following the Sunday morning service, the minister requested Dr. Van Til to come to the front of the sanctuary. He did, and was presented with a large, leather-bound album of art, containing classic illustrations done by the masters.

He stood before the congregation, tears trickling down his cheeks, speechless.

People said it was the only time they could remember that the beloved professor had nothing to say except a choked, "Thank you."

CHAPTER 24

"Nobody, But Nobody, Understands Van Til"

No one even slightly acquainted with Dr. Van Til could fail to be impressed with his appreciation of the lighter as well as the more serious aspect of life. "Man is the only creature who laughs and weeps," wrote William Hazlitt. "For he is the only creature who is struck with the difference between what things are and what they ought to be." This is a fair summation of Van Til's philosophy of humor.

No sooner had he begun his teaching career when an incident occurred that endeared him to the students of Princeton Seminary.

An incurable prankster drifted into Van Til's class in junior apologetics before the lecture and placed a thumb tack, point up, on the chair of the student who would be sitting directly in front of him. The latter seminarian had become an enthusiastic advocate of the victorious life movement. He would argue at length that if a follower of Christ would meet certain conditions prescribed in the New Testament he could be delivered from defeatism, worry, discouragement, turmoil, fears, bad temper, in fact all inner tensions.

Presently the victim of the prank strolled into the

classroom and sat squarely on the thumb tack. He
suffered a temporary relapse from his victorious life
conviction, let out a stentorian "Ouch!," jumped
up, and withdrew the tack of torture from his trous-
ers. Full of moral indignation, he wheeled and
flung the thing at the head of the tormentor. The
class, viewing the scenario and aware of its implications, exploded with laughter.

It was several minutes before any semblance of
order was restored. Meanwhile, Van Til stood on
the platform looking very much like a wooden Indian on display. When he had the attention of the
students, he said with the utmost solemnity, "We
shall continue from that *point*."

More moments passed before he could start his
lecture.

This surprisingly versatile man is gifted with the
capacity to assume the role of the comic. At a stunt
night put on by his home church, Van Til put aside
his dignity for the evening and appeared on the
podium as Spartacus. Spartacus was the Thracian
gladiator who led a band of slaves in an uprising
against the Romans in an effort to gain their freedom.

He appeared on the stage, clad in a tin helmet, a
knee-length toga belted with a colorful sash, san-
dals, and bearing a tin sword and an aluminum
plate for a shield. Storming back and forth like a
general before his army, he launched into a passionate, ringing speech, eyes flashing, sword cleav-
ing the air, and throat breathing out threats against
all who would grind him and his followers under-
foot.

Most modern church historians agree that the English Puritans, great and godly people that they were, simply did not have enough fun in life. Lord Macaulay probably exaggerated their stern attitude toward amusement when he charged the Puritans with hating bear-baiting, not because it gave pain to the bear but because it gave pleasure to the spectators. There may be some truth in the barb.

But the Book of Proverbs is filled with subtle wit and humor, and heartily endorses the right kind of enjoyment. "A merry heart doeth good like a medicine"—literally, "is good medicine" (Prov. 17:22). ". . . he that is of a merry heart hath a continual feast" (Prov. 15:15). Said Mr. Spurgeon, himself a humorist of a high order, "I sometimes think there is as much holiness in a laugh as in a cry."

Supersensitive people cannot endure being lampooned or made a target for laughs, nor should they. But a delightful dimension of Cornelius Van Til is his willingness to be put in stocks and pillory if it contributes to wholesome amusement. This came out at a Westminster Seminary banquet, held at the close of a school year, when the master of ceremonies was presenting the good-natured Dutchman.

"There is a controversy today as to who is the greatest intellect of this segment of the twentieth century," the m.c. said. "Probably most thinking people would vote for the learned Dr. Einstein. Not me. I wish to put forth as my candidate for the honor, Dr. Cornelius Van Til." (Loud applause.) "My reason for doing so is this: Only eleven people

in the world understand Albert Einstein. . .
Nobody—but *nobody* in the world—understands
Cornelius Van Til."

And nobody in the banquet hall enjoyed the joke
more than the subject. But revenge is sweet.

One morning the skillful toastmaster, an alumnus of the seminary, was entering Machen Hall, the
administration building, when he happened to run
into Dr. Van Til. "Good morning," he said. "Are
you holding any classes in apologetics today?"

"Not today," said the theologian.

"Too bad," he said. "I'd hoped to sit in and pick
up some pearls of wisdom."

With no hesitation whatever, Van Til replied, "I
don't cast my pearls before swine."

At that, the alumnus bowed and muttered,
"Touché."

CHAPTER 25

Education and Evangelism

Two projects that lie close to the heart of Cornelius Van Til are Christian education and evangelism.

He believes in Christian education for covenant youth, not because he himself is a product of the Christian school, but because knowledge of God is essential to a true grasp of science, history, the arts, social studies—in fact, all culture. Since the triune God is the fountain of life and it is in His light alone that one sees light, it follows that the Lord of creation and providence must interpret His own universe. Man is not autonomous in knowledge, any more than he is autonomous in redemption; therefore, Van Til maintains, he should be "receptively reconstructive." Otherwise how can he possibly think God's thoughts after Him?

Parents in the Christian Reformed Church have formed the vanguard in the matter of organizing Christian School associations, believing that it is the duty of parents, not the church as such, to supervise education. Other Reformed people are following their example. As an encouraging result, more evangelically minded men and women have caught the vision and are busy founding Christian day schools throughout the nation.

Christian education is a logical corollary of covenantal responsibility, an imperative duty that is binding on fathers and mothers who are directed to rear their children in the nurture and discipline of the Lord. Dr. Van Til feels so deeply on this biblical mandate that he often gets carried away propagating the subject.

The teacher of apologetics is no less zealous in support of aggressive evangelism. In God's providence, he has been used to proclaim the gospel on three continents and to demand a reorientation of all of life under the lordship of Christ, not just a simple acceptance of Christ as Savior. David Kucharsky has noted in *Christianity Today* that as a young man Cornelius devoted himself to street preaching in Hammond, Indiana. Former ministers in Calvary Presbyterian Church will attest that in his prime he relished the opportunity to accompany them on sick calls. Quietly and unobtrusively, he used to engage in hospital visitation for the purpose of reading Scripture to and praying for patients. He has been seen in public parks telling Bible stories to children. He particularly enjoys distributing the Scriptures and has supported the Gideons for many years.

According to the Old Testament, venerable Caleb, after a stormy career, had the right to retire from active service. The Israelites came to him and asked him what he wished to do with his remaining years. "Give me Hebron," he said. It was an astonishing request. Hebron, a mountain stronghold, was the dwelling place of the Anakim, or giants. Caleb proceeded to drive them out. Subsequently, Hebron became his inheritance.

In the fall of 1978 Van Til, Jack Miller (a lecturer at Westminster Seminary), Bruce Hunt and Heber McIlwaine (retired missionaries from the Orient), and several young people journeyed to New York City to do street preaching on Wall Street. No heckling from a cross-section of their listeners could stop the men from pressing on the public the claims of King Jesus—this is an unlikely theater of evangelistic effort. Dr. Van Til, a modern Caleb approaching eighty-five, was as vigorous and vital as ever as he boldly held forth the Word of Life, entreating people in Christ's stead to be reconciled to God.

Shortly before ex-President Harry Truman died, he received a letter from 16 Rich Avenue, Philadelphia. The sender placed himself on the same level as the receiver. Both, said Van Til, had certain things in common. Both were now aging. Both were guilt-ridden human beings. In their own righteousness both stood condemned before the judgment bar of a holy God. Both desperately needed the cleansing grace of Jesus, God's only Son, offered up as a sacrifice for sin and raised the third day according to the Scriptures. It was the writer's prayer that Mr. Truman, with him, might be led to the place of true repentance and faith in the Savior.

There was never an acknowledgment of the letter. But certainly when the Judge of the whole earth will bring to light the hidden things of darkness and make manifest the counsels of the heart, the former President, if not among the redeemed, will not be able to say, "I never had the gospel presented to me."

Lately, Van Til has taken a particular interest in reaching the Jewish community with the Good News. One reason for this, he explains, is that, sadly, "interest in Jewish theology and apologetics is not very large in evangelical circles." Another reason is that through the writings of certain modern Jewish scholars, chiefly Martin Buber, the Hassidic Israeli thinker, Jewish philosophy is exercising a subtle but substantial influence on Christian scholarship.

Van Til is aware that post-biblical rabbinical Judaism, which generally follows the currents of modern philosophy, is a far cry from the time of Maimonides (1135–1204). The post-Kantian Jewish writers were as much affected by Kant as were all the philosophers of their time. Because of this, much of Christian evangelism slanted at modern westernized Jewry has fallen on deaf ears. These are folk as much concerned with their own sovereignty and autonomy as any other philosophical group.

Van Til has taken upon himself the task of reading the massive literature of contemporary Judaism. His long-term insights into idealism have helped him sketch out Buber's basic dependence on the I-Thou versus the I-It relationship that runs through a great deal of contemporary liberal theology.

His investigations into Buber have made him conscious of the impact of the Jewish scholar on the formulation of the *Confession of '67,* the revised and watered-down standard adopted by the United

Presbyterian Church (the denomination resulting from the merger of the United Presbyterian Church in North America and the Presbyterian Church in the U.S.A. in 1958). Many are hoping that the former Westminster professor will write more extensively on this relationship in a three-volume work, *Christianity and Conflict,* on which he is currently working.

His pamphlet, *Christ and the Jews,* a brief philosophical treatment of Jewish thought, is an expression of his concern for the Hebrews. With the great apostle, he could say, "My heart's desire and prayer to God for Israel is, that they might be saved" (Rom. 10:1). In *Jerusalem and Athens,* Dr. Paul Jewett, of the Fuller Theological Seminary faculty, both commends and quizzes *Christ and the Jews.* It may be that in *Christianity and Conflict,* Dr. Van Til will deal more comprehensively with some of the questions Jewett poses.

At any rate, the breadth of his vision and the universality of his missionary outreach is becoming increasingly evident to those who follow his writings.

CHAPTER 26

Home Life

"I can never form a correct judgment of a man from seeing him in a religious meeting," theologian Arthur Pink wrote. "He may seem a very splendid person there, and say very beautiful things, but let me go home with him, and there I learn the actual state of the case."

From the start of Van Til's marriage to Rena Klooster in 1925 until God removed her from earth early in 1978, their relationship was an almost unbroken span of sweet companionship.

They lived together as heirs of the grace of life except when, for financial reasons, temporary separations forced them apart while Cornelius taught at Calvin Seminary and other institutions. Rena was always the faithful and industrious wife, an immaculate housekeeper, an uncomplaining mate when shadows gathered. A serene "whither thou goest I will go, and whither thou lodgest I will lodge," characterized her attitude toward her husband, even when it meant sacrificing the beauty of the fields for the ashes of an urban dwelling.

On his part, Cornelius adored her, leaned heavily on her, delighted to be with her. Unless illness or absence from town prevented, they were never absent from the house of worship. It was an inspiration for both minister and members of the congregation to see them seated together reverently and radiantly worshiping the God they loved, an aura of sanctity surrounding them. "The hoary head is a crown of glory, if it be found in the way of righteousness" (Prov. 16:31).

The Van Tils were known to be warmhearted hosts. During the spring and summer months they usually entertained callers on the front porch—in the fall and winter seasons in the living room before a crackling fire in the huge fireplace. Mrs. Van Til always served tea or coffee with homemade cake or cookies.

Multiple visitors converted their residence into a kind of hotel. Seminary students and local or out-of-town friends and acquaintances would converge on 16 Rich Avenue for a friendly chat, or to seek advice, or to ask for help on a theological or philosophical problem. The air would sometimes be filled with references to Tillich, Hegel, Plato, or Calvin; Kuyper, Bavinck, Hepp, Stoker, Dooyeweerd, or Clark; Buswell, Schaeffer, Pinnock, or Montgomery. At other times, in that relaxed atmosphere where formality had no place, conversation flowed easily and naturally, puzzling questions found answers, occasionally doubts were dissolved. "Ointment and perfume rejoice the heart: so doth the sweetness of a man's friend by hearty counsel" (Prov. 27:9).

The Dutch are not a terribly demonstrative people, but their piety is free from artifice. Both

Rena and Cornelius had been reared in a climate of godliness. Their parents had bequeathed to them true riches. The Bible was their chart and compass, directing their steps into paths of quiet holiness. Family worship was as natural to them as breathing. Meals were opened with supplication and ended with thanksgiving. They sought to meditate on the Word of God night and day. The candle of the Lord shone upon their home and the Spirit of the living Savior anointed their heads with oil. Friends of theirs will tell you it was like a benediction to have been with them.

When Earl Van Til, the son of Cornelius and Rena, was growing up, Cornelius nursed a powerful longing to see Earl follow in his father's footsteps, professionally. On finishing high school, the son attended Calvin College and majored in philosophy, trying earnestly to interest himself in it. It never worked out. Earl felt that God had been pleased to withhold the gifts poured out on his father and instead had given him a mind with a scientific bent.

Eventually, the father came to recognize the hand of God in the matter of his son's vocation. He cheerfully accepted the result, and interpreted Earl's decision as the working out of God's will.

Upon graduation from Calvin, Earl accepted a position where he might apply his talents. He married a fine young lady, Thelma Greiner, a member of Glenside Orthodox Presbyterian Church, and together they have established a strong Christian home. They have been active in the work of the church ever since their marriage. Their only child,

Sharon, studied at Geneva College, married Larry
Reid, and now resides in western Pennsylvania.

Late in 1977, Rena Van Til, as the result of an
accident, was hospitalized. Following the accident,
she sustained a severe stroke. During her illness,
Dr. Van Til visited her daily at the Chestnut Hill
Hospital. He would read the Bible, pray with her,
and sing some of the great hymns from the Trinity
Hymnal. The songs were, he says, a source of tremendous comfort.

On January 11, 1978, God summoned her into
His presence. After fifty-three years of happiness
blended with much sorrow and disappointment,
the silver cord that bound them together snapped.

Epilogue

It is early afternoon in suburban Philadelphia.

The silver-haired octogenarian dons his old felt hat and overcoat. He has finished his tea at the well-worn kitchen table covered with oilcloth. He steps out the back door of his home and proceeds along the tiny street that has only three houses. He walks briskly over the lawns. Neighbors wave at him and voice respectful greetings. He exchanges nice comments about their flowers and vegetables.

Between snatches of conversation, the tendrils of his mind reach out in contemplation of Abraham, Moses, Isaiah, of God's own Son, of Paul, Tertullian, Athanasius, Calvin, Schiller, Vos, Kuyper, Machen—abstracts absorbed from two thirds of a century of concentrated study.

Behind the houses on Rich Avenue there is a retirement home for Roman Catholic priests and nuns. Van Til is a figure well-known to the residents. He enjoys the spacious grounds, the luxuriant lawns fringed with flower beds and dotted with wooden benches. He also enjoys talking with the nuns and the priests, and they with him. They know his theology, and he theirs.

Presently, he strikes up a conversation with another visitor to the grounds. Van Til invites him to go into the main building and shows him the huge Byzantine-like mosaic of the glorified Redeemer. They stand thoughtfully before the mosaic. Van Til drops asides about the final triumph of the believer in Christ.

As the sun races toward the western horizon, the retired professor returns home. A young seminary couple is living with him. The seminarian's wife has prepared the dinner.

He spends the evening in his study reading Scripture and engaging in his current writing.

His posture is curiously reminiscent of the Spanish artist Murillo's concept of Augustine at his desk. Against a dark backdrop, Augustine sits with upturned face, a hand holding a quill poised over an open book. Off to the side the other hand is extended as though to receive an invisible gift.

The face is singularly animated, eager, expectant.

APPENDIX 1

Outline of the Van Til Apologetic[1]

A. My problems with the "traditional method."*
   1. This method compromises God himself by maintaining that his existence is only "possible" albeit "highly probable," rather than ontologically and "rationally" necessary.
   2. It compromises the counsel of God by not understanding it as the only all-inclusive, ultimate "cause" of whatsoever comes to pass.
   3. It compromises the revelation of God by:
      a. Compromising its *necessity*. It does so by not recognizing that even in Paradise man had to interpret the general (natural) revelation of God in terms of the convenantal obligations placed upon him by God through special revelation. Natural revelation, on the traditional view, can be understood "on its own."
      b. Compromising its *clarity*. Both the general and special revelation of God are said to be unclear to the point that man may say only that God's existence is "probable."

---

*Van Til speaks here of the classic, historic attempts to prove the existence of God, derived primarily from Roman Catholicism—and especially Aquinas—but still widely used even by evangelicals.

[1]*The Reformed Pastor and the Defense of Christianity & My Credo*, Presbyterian and Reformed Publishing Co., Box 185, Nutley, New Jersey, 07110. Used by permission.

      c. Compromising its *sufficiency*. It does this by allowing for an ultimate realm of "chance" out of which might come "facts" such as are wholly new for God and for man. Such "facts" would be uninterpreted and unexplainable in terms of the general or special revelation of God.

      d. Compromising its *authority*. On the traditional position the Word of God's self-attesting characteristic, and therewith its authority, is secondary to the authority of reason and experience. The Scriptures do not identify themselves, man identifies them and recognizes their "authority" only in terms of his own authority.

4. It compromises man's creation as the image of God by thinking of man's creation and knowledge as independent of the Being and knowledge of God. On the traditional approach man need not "think God's thoughts after him."

5. It compromises man's covenantal relationship with God by not understanding Adam's representative action as absolutely determinative of the future.

6. It compromises the sinfulness of mankind resulting from the sin of Adam by not understanding man's ethical depravity as extending to the whole of his life, even to his thoughts and attitudes.

7. It compromises the grace of God by not understanding it as the necessary prerequisite for "renewal unto knowledge." On the traditional view man can and must renew himself unto knowledge by the "right use of reason."

B. My understanding of the relationship between Christian and non-Christian, philosophically speaking.

1. Both have presuppositions about the nature of reality:
   a. The Christian presupposes the triune God and his redemptive plan for the universe as set forth once for all in Scripture.
   b. The non-Christian presupposes a dialectic between "chance" and "regularity," the former accounting for the origin of matter and life, the latter accounting for the current success of the scientific enterprise.
2. Neither can, as finite beings, by means of *logic* as such, say what reality *must* be or *cannot* be.
   a. The Christian, therefore, attempts to understand his world through the observation and logical ordering of facts in self-conscious subjection to the plan of the self-attesting Christ of Scripture.
   b. The non-Christian, while attempting an enterprise similar to the Christian's, attempts nevertheless to use "logic" to destroy the Christian position. On the one hand, appealing to the *non-rationality* of "matter," he says that the chance-character of "facts" is conclusive evidence against the Christian position. Then, on the other hand, he maintains like Parmenides that the Christian story cannot possibly be true. Man must be autonomous, "logic" must be legislative as to the field of "possibility" and possibility must be above God.
3. Both claim that their position is "in accordance with the facts."
   a. The Christian claims this because he interprets the facts and his experience in the light of the revelation of the self-attesting Christ in Scripture. Both the uniformity and the diversity of

facts have at their foundation the all-embracing plan of God.
   b. The non-Christian claims this because he interprets the facts and his experience in the light of the autonomy of human personality, the ultimate "givenness" of the world and the amenability of matter to mind. There can be no fact that denies man's autonomy or attests to the world's and man's divine origin.
4. Both claim that their position is "rational."
   a. The Christian does so by claiming not only that his position is self-consistent but that he can explain both the seemingly "inexplicable" amenability of fact to logic and the necessity and usefulness of rationality itself in terms of Scripture.
   b. The non-Christian may or may not make this same claim. If he does, the Christian maintains that he cannot make it good. If the non-Christian attempts to account for the amenability of fact to logic in terms of the ultimate rationality of the cosmos, then he will be crippled when it comes to explaining the "evolution" of men and things. If he attempts to do so in terms of pure "chance" and ultimate "irrationality" as being the well out of which both rational man and a rationally amenable world sprang, then we shall point out that such an explanation is in fact no explanation at all and that it destroys predication.
C. My proposal, therefore, for a consistently Christian methodology of apologetics is this:
   1. That we use the same principle in apologetics that we use in theology: the self-attesting, self-explanatory Christ of Scripture.
   2. That we no longer make an appeal to "common

notions" which Christian and non-Christian agree on, but to the "common ground" which they actually have because man and his world are what Scripture says they are.

3. That we appeal to man as man, God's image. We do so only if we set the non-Christian principle of the rational autonomy of man against the Christian principle of the dependence of man's knowledge on God's knowledge as revealed in the person and by the Spirit of Christ.

4. That we claim, therefore, that Christianity alone is reasonable for men to hold. It is wholly irrational to hold any other position than that of Christianity. Christianity alone does not slay reason on the altar of "chance."

5. That we argue, therefore, by "presupposition." The Christian, as did Tertullian, must contest the very principles of his opponent's position. The only "proof" of the Christian position is that unless its truth is presupposed there is no possibility of "proving" anything at all. The actual state of affairs as preached by Christianity is the necessary foundation of "proof" itself.

6. That we preach with the understanding that the acceptance of the Christ of Scripture by sinners who, being alienated from God, seek to flee his face, comes about when the Holy Spirit, in the presence of inescapably clear evidence, opens their eyes so that they see things as they truly are.

7. That we present the message and evidence for the Christian position as clearly as possible, knowing that because man is what the Christian says he is, the non-Christian will be able to understand in an intellectual sense the issues involved. In so doing, we shall, to a large extent, be telling him what he "already knows" but seeks to suppress. This "re-

minding" process provides a fertile ground for the Holy Spirit, who in sovereign grace may grant the non-Christian repentance so that he may know him who is life eternal.

APPENDIX 2

This talk was presented in Grace Chapel, Reformed Episcopal Church, Philadelphia, Pennsylvania, in March, 1969, to a gathering of interested laymen and students meeting at the invitation of the Mid-Atlantic Chapter of the Association for the Advancement of Christian Scholarship. It is a verbatim transcription of the words and phrases with which Dr. Van Til has presented his Credo all through the years and it represents his views as only he can present them.

We are to think together tonight of those who have helped us to have a broader and deeper insight of the work of Christ in our behalf than we, without them, would have had. We are to think particularly of the fact that they have helped us to see something more of Christ as the Lord of history than we, without them, would have had.

When Christ was on earth He said that He had come to bring unto men the kingdom of heaven. And who would enter into that kingdom of heaven? Only the pure in heart. If men would enter into that kingdom they must be holy even as God is holy. "Be ye therefore perfect as your Father in heaven is perfect."

But who is perfect? No man is perfect. The heart of man is deceitful and desperately wicked, who can know it? Who can cleanse it? Only Christ. "Whoso eateth my flesh, and drinketh my blood, hath eternal life; and I will raise him up at the last day." Only he that is born from above, born again by the Spirit, can see the kingdom of heaven. So then salvation is and must be the gift of the grace of God.

And if eternal life is the gift of grace given by the triune God, then this gift must be preserved in this world till the end of time against the wiles of the devil. And the devil operates everywhere. Knowing that Christ has wrested the kingdoms of the world from him, he fights a war of desperation in order to do as much damage as he can to Christ, the rightful King of the world and to those who are enlisted in His cause. There is therefore a war to the death between Christ and Satan for allegiance of man. Christ has assigned to His followers the task of breaking down the works of darkness everywhere. These works must be broken down *absolutely*. The soldiers of Christ must give no quarter to the enemies of Christ. And as they are on their daily search-and-destroy mission, this mission must begin with the daily cleansing of their own hearts.

In all this, however, the followers of Christ must never doubt the final victory of Christ their King. The future is theirs because they are Christ's.

[Noah, the Man of God]

Look now how some of the servants of Christ that have gone before have helped us to see the meaning of the words, "Christ is Lord of history."

There was Noah, the man of God. Christ's work of saving His people from their sins, was, as it seemed, about to stop. *All* men had corrupted their ways. The judgment simply must come. The God of holiness can no longer bear the sight of man, but Noah found grace in

God's sight. So Noah walked with God. Before men he kept the law of God. So he was a preacher of righteousness before ever speaking a word to men. Noah is assigned the task of building an ark. When the ark is built, he and his family are told to enter into it. They must be preserved. How else can Christ perform His work of saving His people from their sin?

[Noah's Dialogue]

And now while abuilding the ark Noah engages in dialogue with his carpenters. "We like you, Mr. Noah. You give us good wages. You treat us well. But please tell us why you are building this ark." Noah tells them that God has appeared to him and has told him that a flood is coming to destroy all sinners from the earth. Let them repent! God is still *enduring* them, *calling* them to Himself while the ark is abuilding.

Then one of their spokesmen said: "Surely, Noah, as a sensible man you must realize that nobody can know anything about the beyond. You must not expect us, as reasonable men, to listen to you when you speak thus wildly about knowing what ultimate reality is all about. You tell us that a flood will come to destroy us all. You connect this flood of yours with our sins. Then you trace this sin back to our supposed first ancestor to whom your God is also supposed to have spoken. Thus you offer us a philosophy of origins as well as a philosophy of the future on the basis of this dream of yours.

"What evidence could you possibly give us to prove that God has really spoken to you? If you want to convince us of the fact that this revelation of yours is genuine, you will have to offer us an entire philosophy of history, one that is intelligible to us in terms of principles that spring from our experience. We have learned that for the interpretation of our experience we need both the idea of a wholly determined and of a wholly open universe. We need both of these ideas in order to account for the measure of order or permanence that we see within and about us and for the measure of newness or contingency that we see within and about us. If we took either of these ideas by itself, then we would have either a wholly static or a wholly moving reality. So we take these ideas as limiting or supplementative concepts one of another.

"On the basis of this—our combination of two principles of pure rationalism and pure irrationalism—we can at least be sure that what you say about your God having created the world and having thus related the I-It dimension, the dimension of rain and sunshine, to the I-thou dimension, to the dimension of moral right and wrong so that He can not only predict the coming of a flood but actually cause it to come (and that for our sins), is impossible. Of course, we have taught our children the story of our great, great grandfather, and of his fall into sin. But we have, at the same time demythologized this tale. How unethical it would be to say that *because* of our *biological* relation to Adam we are *ethically* involved in sin. Surely to think in truly ethical fashion we must think of each man as standing where this legendary Adam is supposed to have stood—namely, as absolutely autonomous in his choice for good or evil. Then, as to the future, we do not pretend to be able to predict what may come forth from the womb of chance. But one thing we are certain cannot happen, or the universe would be utterly immoral.

"No flood will come *because* of what you call our sin. And so far as evidence is concerned, there are no records within the memory of man of any flood that covered the highest mountains."

[Noah's Farewell Address]

Then Noah made one final farewell address to his contemporaries: "My friends, I am deeply grieved for your sakes. You and I apparently serve different gods. My God controls all that can possibly come to pass. Your god is a god that floats about in pure metaphysical abstract possibility. My God is self-determinate and *therefore* created the ordinances of the world in which we live. He assigned to Adam, the father of us all, the task of subduing the earth. Through him He gave us all a mandate with respect to whatever we do, whether we eat or drink or do anything else. We are to do it all to His praise. In this mandate every fact in the I-It dimension offers us an opportunity of serving Him. He has asked us that we be prophets, priests, and kings under Him and unto Him. But we have even in Him as our representative broken this arrangement, this order, this covenant in which He had placed us all. We all have broken His covenant by day and by night. We have broken His covenant in every dimension or aspect of life.

"But God will not be defeated by man. He promised Adam that the seed of the woman should bruise the head of the seed of the serpent. There *will* be, there *must* be, a complete destruction of evil in this world. God is therefore going to destroy the present world with a flood. He is determined upon a radical cleansing of the world in order then to build it anew. He can do so because the future is wholly in His hand. If you would be saved from destruction, you must repent for having broken the ordinances of God everywhere they confronted you. And they confront you everywhere. I, myself, have repented. I am telling you all this on His authority. You say that you want proof of His existence as the All-Determining One. But surely without this God speaking to you with authority, you must yourself be your own authority. When you speak about the past and about the future, you know that you don't control them. You know that if what I told you about God's revelation to me is not true, because He says it, then what you say is true must be true, because *you* say it. Between you and God there remains nothing but a test of strength. Repent and believe ere it be too late. See how all your words of opposition to God about the past, the present, and the future presuppose the fact of God and of His work of creation and redemption in the world. Your own mouths condemn you. Repent and believe ere it be too late."

[Jesus and the Pharisees]

Look now for just a moment at Jesus and His conversation with the Pharisees. Jesus claims that He is one with the Father. He forgives their sins even as He heals their bodies. He stills the storms on the sea of Galilee. He is preparing a people that will be truly holy and therefore truly fit for the kingdom of heaven. And He gives them a foretaste of the new heaven and the new earth on which righteousness will dwell by the miracles He performs.

Then He has dialogue with the Pharisees. They say He blasphemes when He makes Himself out to be the Son of God. They say there can be only one God, and there can be no absolute manifestation of this one God on earth. Everything temporal is relative. Even the law of Moses must be interpreted according to the ever-expanding ethical consciousness of man. If Jesus wants to prove His divinity, He must do so by subordinating His claims to Messiahship to the demands of this growing ethical consciousness of man.

Over against this position of the Pharisees, Jesus did what He had enabled His servant Noah to do. He sought no credentials anywhere outside Himself. He identified Himself as the direct revelation of God in the I-It dimension. He challenged the Pharisees to interpret Moses and all that he had said about the origins of God for man and of the whole cosmos in terms of His [Jesus'] authority. He says that they, though "experts" in Moses and the prophets, had wholly misunderstood them. And would they know about the future? Then they better ask Him about it. He alone knew the outcome of all things. He would be their judge at last.

The Pharisees clung to their covenant-breaking philosophy of man and of history. They held to it as stubbornly as the men of Noah's day had held to their opposition. Both did so in order to rationalize their wicked deeds. They were so sure they were right that they crucified Jesus who was the Way, the Truth, and the Life. They thought they were victorious when they had nailed Him to the cross. In reality it was He who was victorious over them. When He said, "It is finished," it *was* finished. Satan and his hosts were vanquished. The gates of hell would be unable henceforth to obstruct the coming of the kingdom of heaven in any final way. The whole earth is subject now to Jesus Christ as King. A mighty army, the army of God, goes forth to battle now. In the spirit of Noah, but with deeper consciousness of the meaning of the struggle between Christ and Satan, they now rejoice in the fact that they may follow in the all-conquering train. On their escutcheon the words *Pro Rege* are emblazoned. Looking at the cross of Christ, they cry out, "In this sign conquer."

Peter and Paul were soon to show themselves fearless before the Sanhedrin in the defense of their King. They would proclaim the only name given under heaven by which men must be saved. They looked forward toward that regeneration of all things of which their Lord had spoken while He walked with them in Galilee.

[The City of God]

The Holy Spirit will lead His church, His people, into all the truth. As time goes on they will understand more and more of the depth and of the breadth of the program of redemption that was initiated and is directed by Christ. The Commander in Chief sits enthroned in glory now. He has given them His Word to direct them. He has given them His Spirit to enlighten and to quicken them. They have put on the whole armor of God in order to do battle with the powers of darkness. Satan still claims the whole universe for his domain. When man seeks to investigate first or last being, behold Satan is there to insinuate that he must, in doing so, never betray the principle of his own inward self-sufficiency. It is this that Satan had insinuated into the hearts of Adam and of Eve. When anyone claims to come to him with a revelation from God, then he must ask of him his credentials and for the credentials of his God. Fully in the service of Satan, Socrates expressed this idea when he said that the good must be good because he can himself, without reference to what gods or men say about it, see it to be good.

The god of Socrates, the god of Plato and of Aristotle, following Socrates, can say nothing about the past, the present, or the future. This god is made in man's image and is therefore of no more help to man than the god Dagon was to the Philistines when it was confronted with the ark of the Lord. This god was like the god of the Pharisees and the god of the Pharisees was like this god. It was an abstract principle of unity projected by man. This abstract principle of unity was unity only when it was thought of as *negatively* related to the world of space and time. When this god of negative unity was thought of as related to the world of space and time then it was thought of as correlative to space and time. And being thus correlative to space and time, this unity became immersed in plurality. And this plurality was the plurality of pure chance or contingency. The man who manufactured this scheme of abstract unity correlative to abstract plurality was destroyed by it as by a Frankenstein monster. The man who constructs this monster is supposed to know himself before he has constructed it and yet is also to understand himself in the light of it. The man who must think of himself as being what he is in terms of the form-matter scheme of Greek philosophy must think of himself as moving upward toward absorption into abstract form and downward into absorption into abstract contingency.

It was in this sort of philosophy, as comprehensively expressed by Plotinus, that Augustine was brought up. By means of it he had sought to answer skepticism and dualism. Surely no pure plurality can have any meaning, he said. One must have a principle of comprehensive unity. And here it is. Plato and Plotinus had maintained their own personal autonomy and had set forth a philosophy that gave unity to experience.

Then the Holy Spirit worked upon Augustine's heart. He heard in the garden the word *tolle lege,* and he read. By reading the Scriptures, he found the Christ. He learned to interpret himself in terms of the Christ who had defied the Pharisees when He had said that though He spake of Himself yet He knew that what He said was true. He [Augustine] knew that man was not participant in deity, as the Greeks said he was. Man is a creature of God. Man must love and obey God as his Creator. He knew that he was a sinner against the holy will of God. Augustine prostrated himself at the foot of the Cross. "In this sign conquer," conquer first yourself and then the world.

The principle of abstract unity in the world was now no longer some abstract unity contrasted negatively with the principle of plurality abstract unity in the world. The principle of unity in the world was now the operation of the counsel of God with respect to the world. The principle of individuality was now the same counsel of God. The facts of the world were what they were because of this same plan of God with respect to the world. And as for man's cultural task, it was now the interpretation of the plan of God as expressed in the world always under the direction of the redemptive relation of God to man in Christ set forth in Scripture and always in dependence upon the guidance of the Spirit of God.

Now then Augustine was ready to construct his philosophy of history and by means of it to challenge the philosophy of history that he had inherited from the Greeks. There are two cities, he said, the city of God and the city of the world. There are citizens of the city of God and citizens of the city of the world. Their origin is different. Their history is different. Their consummation will be different. Augustine now sees himself to be a creature made in the image of God, a sinner who has broken the ordinances of God, a sinner saved by grace through the blood of Christ. He now stands with Christ, against the Pharisees and against Plotinus, against the contemporaries of Noah.

Here are two kinds of people with different origins, different histories, and different consummations. How then have they any contact with one another? How can the children of light speak to the children of darkness and be understood by them in any sense?

Oh, well Augustine knows that all men are of one stock. He knows that they have all things in common as gifts of God. But it is the use that each makes of these gifts that makes them to differ. The difference between them is ethical, not metaphysical or physical. And even the ethical difference is one of principle only. The citizens of the kingdom of heaven must be always ready to confess that what they have in the way of understanding and living by the truth, is the gift of the grace of God. As they seek to destroy evil and seek to do it absolutely, they must always anew begin with the remaining wickedness of their as yet sinful hearts. They must also see the relatively good things that are in the citizens of the kingdom of the world. They are absolutely evil, but they are this in principle only and not fully in degree. They will not be fully evil in degree till the end of the road.

[The Dialogue]

How deeply conscious Augustine was of the fact that to be translated from the kingdom of darkness to the kingdom of light involves a tremendous internal struggle. In particular it involved a tremendous struggle for him, filled as he was with the urge to see life whole and see it through. Augustine [could] not live without a comprehensive philosophy of history. How long and how hard he struggled to overcome within himself that false philosophy of history that he had inherited from the Greeks. What a terrible struggle it was within himself to really listen to the voice of Christ and then to spread out the wings of his mind still following Christ, as he looked backward to the origin of all things and forward to the end of all things. Everywhere Satan seemed to be ahead of him. Everywhere he must drive out Satan and stake his claim in the name of Christ his King. He was not finished with this task when his Lord brought him to the consummation of his own individual life. Much territory remained to be conquered.

[Luther]

In one sense there was no more territory to be claimed for Christ. Augustine had claimed all of reality for Christ. But it was the work of a pioneer that Augustine performed. The Reformers went out to survey the land that Augustine had claimed for Christ. They erected dwelling places there. The enemy had not been fully driven out. They operated in the way the Viet Cong operates in Viet Nam. The citizens of the kingdom of the world proposed a coalition government, and, alas, the citizens of the city of God accepted the proposal.

Till Luther came. In a great struggle, similar to the struggle of Augustine, Luther first cleared the enemy from his own heart. Herewith he marked the beginning of a new offensive. Then Calvin came. He claimed not only the heart of man but the whole of nature and history anew for his King. He repainted the signs that Augustine had first painted. They were scarcely readable any more. He insisted that it is Christ who must tell man what the facts of nature and of history are. It is not man who must interpret these facts and conclude that there is back of them some sort of God. Romanism had allowed Aristotle to claim the realm of nature and of history for Satan. Calvin reclaimed them for Christ. He called upon the soldiers of Christ his King to drive out from their lurking places the followers of the kingdom of this world. In short, he showed them that they must daily bow in deep humility before their Maker and Redeemer and then go on to do all things *coram deo.* All of the activities of the followers of Christ must be acts of service unto Christ. All of life must be religious. He showed that all men make all of life religious in any case. Whether they eat or drink or do anything else, they either serve a false god or the true God. Therefore Calvin called for a renewed consecration to Christ and to a renewed consciousness of the fact that every day and at every point of human interest the struggle for Christ against Satan must be carried on.

[Abraham Kuyper]

Many years went by. The enemy returned again. There was not one sector of the city of God that was immune to his attack. When Israel of old intermarried with the nations they had been called upon to drive out of the land of Canaan, they brought the displeasure of their covenant God upon them. So even the Reformation churches compromised the claims of Christ with the claims of Greek philosophy. To be sure, the Lord was not denying Himself. For Abraham his servant's sake He kept the covenant with His people and preserved a remnant for Himself.

And then there blossomed forth new life out of this remnant. A young student of Leiden University was studying under Dr. J. H. Scholten, a disciple of Friedrich Hegel. Scholten was a fascinating teacher. Young Kuyper was a precocious, brilliant student and a diligent worker. He absorbed the teachings of his master. He seemed to see a marvelous synthesis between Christ and Hegel. But yet, as was true with Augustine, his heart was restless till it rested in the Christ of Scripture.

And what of history? He was about to write a doctoral dissertation on the Polish Reformer A Lasco. But where find the works of A Lasco? He wrote to several university libraries. None had the works of A Lasco. Then he visited a humble pastor, a friend of his father's. This pastor had all the works of A Lasco neatly arranged on his shelves. Is such an event as this to be explained in terms of the form-matter scheme of the Greeks or by the prin-

ciple of the Absolute realizing Himself somehow in the
course of history taking mankind up into itself? No, this
is the work of the Providence of the God of the covenant.
And then he read *The Heir of Redcliffe*, a novel of British
life. In this story he saw the true nature of the church as
from the cradle to his grave it enveloped its members
with the grace of God. After he preached to his country
congregation one day a woman refused to shake hands
with him after the service. His conscience troubled him.
He had been eloquent. He had preached a marvelous
synthesis sermon, but he had not preached Christ.
When he came to see Pietje Balthuis she told him so.
Later, he placed a picture of her above his desk, and it
remained there for the rest of his life.

Now then to work said Abe to himself, and work he
did. He must control the whole history of the church. He
must see the history of the church in relation to human
culture. He studied the lineaments of the self-iden-
tifying Christ of Scripture as these were etched in ever
clearer and deeper lines upon his mind and heart. His
love for this Christ became his one absorbing passion.
This love for Christ burned as ardently when he read
science and philosophy as when he read theology. Augustine was right. Calvin was right. But we must go
beyond both of them in signalizing the fact that
everywhere and with respect to every fact in science and
in philosophy there is a struggle going on between
Christ and Satan. The followers of Christ must not with-
draw from the struggle as the Anabaptists did. They
must not allow for a neutral no-man's land in the field of
science and philosophy as the Roman Catholics did. He
wrote a three volume work under the title *Pro Rege*.

Pro Rege must be the battle cry of those who by the
Spirit of God have been born again and have therefore
seen all things for what they are and in their right rela-

tion to Christ the King. The citizens of the kingdom of God must ever realize that anything basic they say about any fact will be said to be false by the citizens of the kingdom of the world. The citizens of the kingdom of man hate God and hate the believers in Christ. They want to destroy all the markings that the citizens of the kingdom of God have made in behalf of their king, whether these markings be in the field of science, the field of philosophy or the field of theology. Paul says the natural man will always hold under the truth of God in unrighteousness. He will always do what the men of Noah's time did with respect to the words of God that Noah spoke to them. Men of the world will insist that no fact can be what the citizens of the kingdom of God, speaking on the basis of the Word of Christ, say that it is. The citizen of the kingdom of this world comes to the examination of any fact that stands before him by means of a philosophy of history that he has adopted in advance. The citizen of the kingdom of this world is the man with yellow glasses cemented to his eyes. He sees every fact that the citizen of the kingdom of God sees, but he sees them all as centering around man as the ultimate interpreter of them. He sees them as a man who stands on his head sees the facts but sees them topsy turvy.

What then of dialogue between the citizen of the kingdom of the world and the citizen of the kingdom of heaven? Well, as with Augustine and as with Calvin, so Kuyper of course appeals to the fact that all men are created in the image of God. None of them can, therefore, escape the revelation of God—as this speaks to them, round about them, and within them. In this sense all men *know God* and all men know that, as sinners, they are breaking the ordinances of God. But in addition to that, and in this point Kuyper makes a definite step in advance of Augustine and even of Calvin, God gives to them His general, His restraining grace. Calvin taught common grace, but he had not clearly interwoven it with his philosophy of history. Because of the fact that all men everywhere receive the blessings of common grace they do not work out the principle of evil that is within them to its full extent. Even the citizens of the kingdom of this world have not only the wherewithal but also the inclination to subdue the earth. Oft-times they, more than the children of God, make great discoveries in the field of science. They use the discoveries of science for the healing of the diseases of mankind. They form organizations which seek for "justice" and "righteousness" among men as over against those who seem to be doing only evil continually. And in all this they may be said to be helping the citizens of the kingdom of heaven as they carry out the cultural mandate as assigned to them anew in Christ. Nor is all this hypocrisy. For all that, it remains true that their hearts are not right with God. Their goal is not the glory of God. Their standard of action and of thought is not the expressed will of God. Their attitude remains that of the men of Noah's time. They are still, in the last analysis, the servants of Satan. The citizen of the kingdom of heaven will, therefore, gladly accept the good things that are brought forth from the bowels of God's earth by those who do not with them serve the Lord Christ. They will gladly receive help from the citizens of the kingdom of this world as they fulfil! the cultural mandate. They will make use of the services of those who are not of God's people in the way that Solomon made use of those who hewed for him the cedars of Lebanon. Solomon was willing to make much use of all the skills of the Zidonians who were not of the covenant of God, but he insisted that the temple be built according to the blueprint that was shown him on the mount.

Kuyper matched his theoretical insights with his boundless energy in connection with the application of his ideals to actual life. He worked endlessly for the renovation of Christian life in his own country.

In the first place the church must be reformed along genuinely Protestant and Reformed lines. The church must teach its members what true religion is, a deep inward conviction on the part of every one of its members that he has been redeemed from death by the blood of Christ. The church must not repress the true inwardness and the true immediacy of religious conviction in its members.

The church must teach her members not only to express their religious convictions within the institutional bounds of the church but in organizations formed freely outside the church. There must be independent educational societies. There must be a society to develop Christian education for children. A society must be formed for the organization of a Christian university. Up and down the land Kuyper went to enlighten the people, not only the intelligentsia but the common people too, on this important task. When under his inspiration the Free University of Amsterdam was organized, he wrote for it a set of principles called *Reformed Principles.* These principles were not simply the Confessions of the Reformed churches; they discussed the principles of education more directly than a church Confession could.

Then there was the field of politics. The family is the first unit of human society. The members of the family are also members of the church. Finally the members of the family are members of the state. These three, the family, the church, and the state, are each of them sovereign in their own spheres of interest and responsibility. As the individual in the family and the individual in the church so must the individual in the state be set free from the bondage of Romanism and humanism. All three of them must be set free into the liberty wherewith Christ has made them free. Up and down the land, Kuyper went giving public lectures in order to form the antirevolutionary party in politics. The French revolution had for its battle cry, *No God, no master*. We must have for our battle cry, *Pro Rege*.

Imagine then a country dotted with Christian day schools and high schools in which the children of the common people have their covenant consciousness developed during the week days in the field of education as well as on Sundays in the church. Imagine these children growing up, taking their place in society, taking their children with them to hear the preaching of ministers who were stirring up their covenant consciousness at the more advanced levels.

"This is," says Reverend Holkeboer, "the Sunday before election day. Next Tuesday you will be offered the inestimable privilege as free men in Christ to choose certain men for political office. Be sure to vote; it is your duty, it is your privilege. Tomorrow night, the night before the election day, there will be a meeting in our town hall in which Dr. Abraham Kuyper will speak. He will enlighten you as to the possibilities that are before you."

Then imagine Kuyper himself elected to be the prime minister of the land. He leaves his work of teaching of systematic theology at the Free University to his younger colleague, Herman Bavinck, in order to assume this new responsibility. Watch the faces of the members of the second, and later of the first, chamber as they listen to the stream of eloquence that pours forth from the mouth of that broadfaced, determined bigot. But is he a bigot? Listen as this mere theologian speaks wih exhaustive knowledge of the facts on bill number 85. Why the man has even written a two volume work in which he has set forth the principles of his antirevolutionary policy of state!

And watch him as a practical politician. One would think that he would be able to cooperate with nobody. How can he even cooperate with other religious people? At every point he has opposed the Roman Catholics in what they are trying to do in politics as well as in the church, and now he has joined forces with a Roman Catholic faction in the government in order to oppose what he calls our revolutionary policies, the policies of the French Revolution. We have differences among ourselves. We are split up into several groups. But it is high time that we forget our differences for the moment and start a *Stop Kuyper* movement. Long live the French Revolution!

[Off to America]

Meanwhile Kuyper is off to America. He is to give the L. P. Stone lectures at Princeton Theological Seminary.

Speaking in the seminary chapel with such men as B. B. Warfield, Geerhardus Vos, and others of like similar faith and theological stature in the audience, Kuyper ascends the podium. "Is this Napoleon going to the platform," asks one student of another.

"My friends, there is no doubt. . . . that Christianity is imperiled by great and serious dangers. Two life systems are wrestling one with another in mortal combat. Modernism is bound to build a world of its own from the data of the natural man, and to construct man himself from the data of nature; while, on the other hand, all those who reverently bend the knee to Christ and worship Him as the Son of the living God, and as God

Himself, are bent upon saving the 'Christian Heritage.'[1]

"If the battle is to be fought with honor and with a hope of victory, then principle must be arrayed against principle.[2] Now our Christian principle is best expressed in Calvinism. 'In Calvinism my heart has found rest.'[3] What else then but Calvinism could I think of as the proper subject for my lectures here in your midst? 'Calvinism, as the only decisive, lawful, and consistent defence for Protestant nations against encroaching, and overwhelming modernism, . . . this of itself was bound to be my theme.'[4] Let us then speak of Calvinism as a life system. Let us first see how Calvinism is based upon the proper view of man's relation to God. Then let us see how this implies a proper view of man's relation to his fellow man and to the world. Applying this proper insight into the system of truth we discuss Calvinism and Religion, Calvinism and Politics, Calvinism and Science, Calvinism and Art, and Calvinism and the Future."

It is Wednesday evening, dinner time at the seminary club.

"Did you hear the Dutchman these last two afternoons?"

"No, I was too busy studying for a test in apologetics for Brenton Greene."

"Oh, but then you should have heard what the Dutchman said about apologetics. I remember his exact words. It was near the beginning of his first lecture. He was talking about the struggle between two life systems. These Dutchmen borrow everything from the Germans.

---

[1]*Calvinism*, Amsterdam: Hoveker and Wormser, pp. 3-4.
[2]*Ibid.*, p. 4.
[3]*Ibid.*, p. 5.
[4]*Ibid.*

He referred to the German expression *Leben und Weltanschauung:* 'In this struggle, the struggle between systems, apologetics have advanced us not one single step. Apologetics have invariably begun by abandoning assailed breastworks in order to entrench themselves cowardly in a ravelin behind it.'[5]

"What do you suppose he meant? Was he referring to Butler's Analogy? Well, I thought so for a moment. I saw what I thought was a frown on Benny Warfield's face. But then I doubt if he knows much about Butler. He does refer to James Orr, but then Orr's book has a title that is borrowed from the German idea of a world and life view.

"At any rate tomorrow night he is going to speak on Calvinism and Science. I want to hear that lecture. I am told that he believes in a two-fold development of science or even in a science for Christians and a science for non-Christians. That's just like these Calvinists. I've been told that he is a supra-lapsarian Calvinist at that. Surely on the basis of a pure determinism such as these Calvinists hold, there can be no science. And certainly if those who are regenerate have one science and those who are unregenerate have another science, how is there to be dialogue between the two? And if the Christian thinks the non-Christian is totally depraved, and tells him so, there will be not even a moment's confrontation between them. Out with it. I'll have none of it. Please pass the sweet potatoes, Harry, don't keep them all for yourself."

It is Thursday night at the club. "Well, as it turned out, he did come up with his doctrine of a God and his all comprehensive decree. That was for him, he said, the presupposition of the fact of science. And he did not for a moment hide his conviction on the idea of total depravity. But that did not, he said, cut the cables between the

---

[5]*Ibid.,* p. 4.

two classes of people for him at all. He said there was a *common grace* and this restrained men from wickedness.

[Kuyper:] "Indeed, man is incapable of doing any good. Are all unbelievers then wicked and repulsive men? Not at all. In our experience we find that the 'unbelieving world excels in many things. Precious treasures have come down to us from the old heathen civilization. In Plato you find pages that you devour. Cicero fascinates you and bears you along by his noble tone and stirs in you holy sentiments . . . . It is not exclusively the spark of genius or the splendor of talent, which excites your pleasure in the words and actions of unbelievers, but it is often their beauty of character, their zeal, their devotion, their love, their candor, their faithfulness, and their sense of honesty.'[6] Who of us has not been put to the blush by the virtues of the heathen? It is thus a fact, that your dogma of total depravity by sin does not always tally with your experience in life.'[7]

"Well, my friends, by its doctrine of common grace Calvinism can hold on to both what the Bible teaches on human depravity and to what experience teaches about the virtues of the heathen.

"Sin unbridled would have resulted forthwith in the total degeneracy of human life. 'But God arrested sin in its course in order to prevent the complete annihilation of his handiwork, which naturally would have followed.'[8] By his common grace God restrains the working of sin in the natural man. 'By common grace he tames men as wild animals may be tamed and become attractive as domestic animals.'[9]

"Now then even the unbeliever can be of service to us as in Christ we reundertake the original mandate given

---

[6]*Ibid.*, pp. 159–160.
[7]*Ibid.*, p. 160.
[8]*Ibid.*, p. 162.
[9]*Ibid.*, p. 163.

to Adam. 'We see now that history is a coherent process with the Cross as its center, a process in which every nation has its task, and the knowledge of which may be a blessing to every nation.' "[10]

[Back to the students:] "Well, are you going to hear him tomorrow night on art?

"No, but I do want to hear his final lecture on *Calvinism and the Future*. If I were a Calvinist, I would be a horrible pessimist. But I suppose he can make all things come out in the wash by means of his all-embracing decree. As for me I'd rather have a little freedom for myself."

[Kuyper's conclusion:] "My friend, as I now conclude my series of lectures I recall that 'the chief purpose of my lecturing in this country was to eradicate the wrong idea, that Calvinism represented an exclusively dogmatical movement.'[11] Calvinism 'did not stop at a church-order, but expanded in a life-system. . . .'[12] This being the case we exclude 'every idea of imitative repristination.'[13] We must not copy the past as if Calvinism were a petrafact. We must go back to the living root of the Calvinist plant, clean it, and water it and 'so cause it to bud and to blossom once more, now fully in accordance with our actual life, and with the demands of the times to come.'[14]

"We live in a time of spiritual degeneration. 'The most alarming feature, however, of the present situation is the lamentable absence of that receptivity in our decreased organism, which is indispensable to the effecting of a cure. In the Graeco-Roman world such receptivity did exist; the hearts opened spontaneously to receive the truth. To an even stronger degree this receptivity existed

---

[10]*Ibid.*
[11]*Ibid.*, p. 231.
[12]*Ibid.*
[13]*Ibid.*, p. 232.
[14]*Ibid.*

in the age of the Reformation, when large masses cried for the gospel.'[15]

"If Christianity is to be presented as the hope of the future, then it must be presented to men as a total life and world view. Our enemy has an all encompassing life view. Against the deadly danger of Modernism which surrounds us 'ye Christians cannot successfully defend your Sanctuary, but by placing, in opposition to all this, a life and world view of your own, founded as firmly on the basis of your own principle, wrought out with the same clearness and glittering in an equally logical consistency.'[16] And this is equivalent to a return to Calvinism.[17] Only Calvinism has consistently 'followed out the lines of the Reformation. . . .' This means for our time that we must think out our inheritance systematically.[18] Doing this means also that our heritage must be broadened. 'Philosophy, psychology, aesthetics, jurisprudence, and even the medical and natural sciences, each and all of these, when philosophically conceived, go back to principles, and of necessity even the question must be put with much more penetrating seriousness than hitherto, whether the ontological and anthropological principles that reign supreme in the present method of these sciences are in agreement with the principles of Calvinism, or are at variance with their very essence.'[19]

"Nay, not as though Calvinism as such could do anything to rejuvenate the world. 'Unless God send forth His Spirit, there will be no turn, and fearfully rapid will be the descent of the waters. But you remember the Aeolian Harp which men were wont to place outside their casement, that the breeze might wake its music

---

[15]*Ibid.*, p. 237.
[16]*Ibid.*, p. 261.
[17]*Ibid.*
[18]*Ibid.*, p. 266.
[19]*Ibid.*, p. 267.

into life. . . . Now, let Calvinism be nothing but such an Aeolian Harp—absolutely powerless, as it is, without the quickening spirit of God—still we feel it our God-given duty to keep our harp, its strings tuned aright, ready in the window of God's Holy Sion, awaiting the breath of the Spirit.' ''[20]

[Kuyper's Coworkers]

While Kuyper was thus trying his utmost to make American Christians conscious of the Christ-given task of presenting the *civitas dei* as a totality view of life over against the *civitas terrena* as a totality view of life, his *commilitiones* in Amsterdam were carrying on their work in his spirit.

There was Herman Bavinck, some twenty years Kuyper's junior who had already published most of his monumental work on *Reformed Dogmatics*. This work was written in self-conscious relation to all the philosophical movements of the past and of the present. And with his work on *Philosophy of Revelation* Bavinck was, in effect, refuting Ettienne Gilson's idea that a Protestant philosophy is an inherent impossibility. Basic to Protestantism, says Gilson, is the idea of the Bible as the revelation of God, by which even the world of nature must be interpreted. But philosophy, to be philosophy at all, must begin with human reason. And if Christians want to convince non-Christians of the truth of a Christian philosophy they must do so by showing that the truths about God as revealed in Scripture are, though above, not against reason. Bavinck was not restrained by such reasoning as this from developing a comprehensive interpretation of life with the Christian revelation as its foundation.

[20]*Ibid.*, p. 274.

Then there was Dr. W. Geesink who, at Kuyper's urging, worked up a comprehensive work on *The Ordinances of God* and another on *Reformed Ethics.* For Geesink the ordinances of God were the ordinances that God the Creator and Redeemer of men gave to every aspect of created life.

Finally there was J. Woltjer, who though less prolific in his writing, was perhaps more profound than the others. Writing on the *Ideal and the Real* he analyzed the philosophy of Plato and others by means of a critical analysis from the biblical point of view.

[Kuyper's Death]

It was 1920 now. The old warrior must yield his power to the last enemy, which is death. But by faith he saw his Savior beyond the grave. A mass of people came to the burial. Here was the representative of the queen, M. Th. Heemskerk. So long as it was day, said he, Kuyper labored; now he has entered into his rest. A slight stirring of the multitude. Now comes Colyn, the leader of the revolutionary party. Intense silence reigns. Kuyper led us [he said] as a benighted segment of the nation to a place of liberty. He was the man of the "common people." God's absolute sovereignty over all creation, that is the life-principle of Calvinism. Then comes R. H. Woltjer, rector of the Free University. [Woltjer said] Kuyper became for us the founder of a truly Calvinistic philosophy of life. When Woltjer is seated, Dr. K. Dyk arises to speak of Kuyper's significance for the Reformation of the Church. And at last comes Mr. A.W.F. Idenburg, the intimate friend of Kuyper, particularly in his later years. "To be near unto God, was Kuyper's personal motto. For him to live was Christ and to die was gain."

Idenberg asked the audience to sing [the metric version of] Psalm 89:15–17: *Hoe zalig is het volk dat naar uw klanken hoort. . . . Gy toch, Gy zyt hun roem de kracht van hunne kracht* [Blessed is the people that know the joyful sound. . . . For you, you are the glory of their strength. . . .].

Then after Dr. H. H. Kuyper, the oldest son of Kuyper had thanked all the audience for their love to his father and they were about to leave, someone in the audience began to sing spontaneously. Soon thousands joined and their singing [of the metric version of Psalm 72:19] was heard afar.

> *Zijn naam moet eewig eer ovangen*
> *nen loof hem vroeg en spa,*
> *De wereld hoor en volg myn zangen*
> *Met Amen, Amen, na.*

> [His name must ever have the praise;
> Let them praise him now and forever.
> Let the world hear and follow my ways,
> With Amen, Amen.]

Soon all the first generation of Kuyper's time began to disappear. No one man could carry on this work.

But little did Kuyper realize that only a few years after his death two brilliant young men would undertake to work out his philosophy of life in much greater detail than he had been able to do.

Drs. D.H.Th. Vollenhoven and Herman Dooyeweerd undertook their work at Amsterdam in 1926. With the deep conviction that the vision Kuyper had seen was their vision too, they began their labors. With the conviction that much territory remained to be won for Christ, they set to work. They worked, as P. Veenhof says, *in Kuyper's line*. They saw that a true philosophy not only is possible on the basis of Reformation principles, but they added that a true philosophy was possible *only* on Reformation principles.

The philosophy of the *civitas terrena* cannot get off the ground. It has bound itself with fetters of iron to the created universe as though it had its explanation in itself. The followers of Augustine, of Calvin and of Kuyper must therefore, obey the vision that Kuyper saw. They must, with whatever reluctance, be as critical of the remnants of scholasticism they find in Kuyper, in Bavinck, in Geesink, and in Woltjer. They must understand that it was difficult for the pioneers in the field of Christian life view to cleanse themselves from the disfiguring detritus of the seaweeds of the deep from which they had emerged.

Then there was the necessity of signalizing the modern post-Kantian form of the *civitas terrena*. The pioneers of a truly Christian philosophy had largely concerned themselves with apostate thinking as it had expressed itself in the Greek form-matter scheme. They had rejected this scheme in the name of the doctrines of creation, fall, and redemption in history through Christ. They had rejected the Roman Catholic synthesis between Christian and Greek principles. So, for instance, Bavinck pointed out with emphasis that the Reformation principle was *ethical* while the scholastic principle was metaphysical. Even so, none of the pioneers had yet fully and exclusively taken their view of man and the world from Scripture. They had not been fully true to the basic principle of the Reformation on this point. They had entered upon the promised land but they had not driven out the Canaanite root and branch from the land.

This fact appeared first of all in their view of man. To be sure, Calvin had expressed, with utmost definiteness the fact that man is what he is because of his relation to God his Creator and to Christ his Redeemer. Many Reformed thinkers after Calvin did not seem to realize that faithfulness to the biblical view would have required the rejection, root and branch, of the Greek notion that man is a *rational animal.* They did not seem to see that this idea of man as a rational animal was indissolubly built into the Greek form-matter scheme of thinking.

Let us then stress, more than our forebears did, the fact that according to the Bible *heart* is the center of man's being. Out of it are the issues of life. Man's intellectual efforts are not neutral at any point. The natural man's heart is desperately wicked. The natural man does not begin to fathom the depth of the wickedness of his own heart. He could not fathom it, even in principle, unless he were redeemed by the blood of Christ and born again by His Spirit, and in that case, he would no longer be the natural man.

One of the first things that needs doing, therefore, is to write a work on the prerogatives and limitation of the intellectual effort of man. In aspostate philosophy man is thought of as participant with God. The laws of thought are therefore thought of as participant in the laws of the divine mind. In this view, logic was thought to be legislative for the nature of all reality. Holding this view, Parmenides, the Greek philosopher, asserted there could be no creation out of nothing. If man is to penetrate the nature of reality by means of his intellect, reality must be a timeless system of being. As a consequence of this view, all of temporal reality was thought of as having no genuine being at all. If this seemed too extreme a position for Plato, then the only thing he could do was to add the principle of pure contingency to that of pure determinism in order thus to obtain some measure of being for the facts and the laws of the world of space and time. And Aristotle, following Plato, and desiring to do *more* justice to temporality than Plato, said that all being has in it both determinism and indeterminism. Being, he said, was analogical. Aristotle did not think of giving up the basic idea of the adequacy of human thought to being as a whole. He was a bit more ready to admit than Plato had been that this ideal of exhaustive interpretation could not be fully attained. But then God could not attain it any more than man. There was always the ultimately irrational beyond both God and man.

It was a sad event when, in the middle ages, Christian theologians, and notably Thomas Aquinas, sought to conjoin this Greek notion of the analogy of being with the Christian notion of the providence of God. And as Kuyper and his coworkers were not able to set themselves altogether free from the evil inheritance of scholasticism with respect to the notion of man so they were not able to set themselves altogether free from this same scholasticism on the matter of the all-comprehensive providence of God. Even in his *Stone Lectures*, Kuyper spoke of some Christian doctrines that were not in dispute between Romanism and Protestantism.

A so-called orthodox Protestant need only mark in his confession and catechism such doctrines of religion and morals as are not subject to controversy between Rome and ourselves, to perceive immediately, that what we have in common with Rome concerns precisely those fundamentals of our Christian creed now most fiercely assaulted by the modern spirit.[21]

It is therefore imperative, argue Vollenhoven and

---

[21]*Ibid.*, p. 252.

Dooyeweerd, that we set our principle of individuation and our principle of unity clearly over against those of Roman Catholic speculation. Kuyper has given us the clue in his concept of sphere-sovereignty. In this doctrine worked out more adequately than it was worked out by Kuyper, we must set forth the biblical views of the relation between individuality and universality in history. All the facts of the universe are created by God and controlled by the all-encompassing providence of God. The whole world is redeemed by Christ. There will be a new heaven and a new earth because of His work. The Holy Spirit regenerates men so that they may see this fact and then gladly undertake anew the cultural mandate given to Adam in paradise for all mankind.

It is thus that the antithetical principle between those who are redeemed by the blood of Christ and those who are of this world is even more sharply expressed by Vollenhoven and Dooyeweerd than it was by Kuyper himself. It was because of the remnants of scholasticism remaining in Kuyper and in his coworkers that they did not altogether escape following the Roman Catholic method of synthesis thinking. And if this was a bad thing in other days how much the more so is it now that modern existentialist methodology controls the thinking of modern humanism.

It was therefore an event of major importance when Vollenhoven wrote his little book on the *Necessity of a Christian Methodology (De Noodzakelyheideener Christelyke Logica)*. In it he shows that the laws of human thought are laws implanted by God in the mind of man as His image bearer, in order that by means of them he might engage in the cultural mandate to subdue the earth. Fallen man assumes that he is not made in the image of God and that the world about him is not created and controlled by God the Creator through Christ the Redeemer. Accordingly, as already noted, apostate man assumes that in order to know reality for what it is he must, by means of the laws of thought, penetrate reality exhaustively. If he cannot penetrate reality exhaustively then, he argues, this reality is not penetrable by a supposed god any more than by man.

[Dialogue]

How then is there to be dialogue between those who are twice born and those who are once born? Is the antithesis between them now made so sharp that the last bit of contact between them is taken away? On the contrary, what formerly remained in the twilight zone is now brought into the open. It is only if the antithesis is so sharply drawn that we can see how the unity is deeper still. In fact, that antithesis could not be so sharply drawn unless the unity between the citizens of the city of God and the citizens of the city of the earth be also clearly drawn.

There would and could be no contact between one man and another man if reality were of the nature that apostate man says that it is. In that case man would be a cross between his participation in a timeless eternal being and his participation in an ocean of pure chance. It is because every man is an image-bearer of God that he cannot escape knowing himself to be other than his apostate principle would require him to be. And it is because the world is what Christ through Scripture says it to be, namely, directed by God as revealed in Christ, that the natural man knows that his philosophy of fact and his philosophy of law cannot be what he, by his adopted principle, must say that they are. Thus it appears that the citizen of the city of God may approach his friends, the citizens of the city of the world, whom he would win unto an allegiance to Christ with utmost confidence of victory. The wisdom of this world has been made foolishness with God. It is thus that Kuyper's vision expanded and clarified by Vollenhoven and Dooyeweerd may help us in our task in undertaking the cultural mandate for ourselves today. Would that more of those who have seen something of Kuyper's vision, as he set it forth in the chapel at Princeton Seminary, might be willing to follow through with Vollenhoven and Dooyeweerd. If they did, they would say, without hesitation, that it is only on the presupposition of the truth of what is taught in Scripture about man and his world, that it is possible for science to understand itself, for philosophy to attain a totality vision that is not a mirage, and for theology to challenge the new Protestant synthesis between Christianity and existentialism and the still newer synthesis of the Aristotle, Christ, Kant axis now functioning in the International Council of the Churches of Christ in the World.